In Stitches

MY TRUE VERSION OF EVENTS

JENNA LEIGH-RAINE

A forty year journey

1

Printed and Bound in United Kingdom. Self-published by CreateSpace.

ISBN-13: 978-1546986119
ISBN-10: 1546986111

First edition. First printing.

Edited by John Price.

Front and back cover Photo Credit: Gloria Eliźee. Artwork credit: Jenna Leigh-Raine

This book is dedicated to those just learning to survive.

CONTENTS

PROLOGUE

When writing this book, I remembered a comment, "Jenna, you went around the world but you have not been away for years." Oh, but I have many times (a psychics code) and seen it all. It's a gift to see, travel and view. Now, I give to you, the reader, ways to at least see how I did it. The book speaks of the CODES to how I survived and created, as I reference (safe houses) to get through, and survive some extreme situations. These codes helped me set myself away from situations that could have blocked, stopped, limited or killed me. The main thing you will take out of this book is that you'll learn not ever imagine to limit yourself. There is one hidden CODE in this book and is up to you to find. If you do, I'll raise my glass to you. Once found you will come to understand 'you never tell'. A clue: "From here I see a runway".

It was a psychic reading I had many years ago that my grandfather William Reginald Davies came through with a message for me, saying I should keep diaries and write. Thank you gramp! It's now a decade since I started out on those diaries.

Up to the age of 35, I had lived more than just the usual everyday existence, but one of designing ways to go forward and more. A life both hard and yet amazing, huge lows and incredible highs. All I ever wanted in life was to be a rock star nothing more. It was age 15 I started to see moving colour images like mini movie clips in my mind. This started happening more frequently, and my school mates and girlfriends were amazed by the detail in readings I produced. Quite soon I knew I was also remote viewing.

To see a person's future was one thing but to view into their energy in real-time, was far more interesting to me. Again this amazed my group of friends and mostly girls at this time. It was a year later I was alone and heard to my left ear the sound of my late Nan calling my name repeatedly. Later my mother explained it was her mother's brother Jo, who was also musical and played the trumpet, possessed the Gift. My life up to this point had been one of many moves to various homes and countries, of which I would have never change.

I didn't enjoy school and to know I was about to leave another one and move on was relief. I recall asking mum "Is this the last one?" I really hated going and with a deep intuitive feeling that school was going to have no baring of my quest to become a star.

Looking back over this book, maybe things were harder than one should go through yet this tells more about the CODES I mentally designed inside to get me through the stages and situations. Now almost 46 I have a silence in my head about my life. I wish it had been easier yet one thing I managed was to never to let my passion for creating music fade. Passion for something you're good at is imperative to self-worth and knowing.

I hope that when you read this book you can feel spirit — the fuel that kept me going. Knowing what makes up who you are, and not what others dictate. "Never Give Up" is just a socially spoken phrase, but to know yourself and belong to you is so important. Freewill is owned by you and no-one else. *In Stitches* are those that I experienced emotionally and physically, and this book will take you on the journey to how, where and when each code was designed. Live, Dream, Survive and Arrive.

I have experienced some incredible times so far in my life and met some of perhaps the most influential stars in music, TV and fashion of my time, including Michael Jackson. Also heroes in music growing up such as Gary Numan, David Sylvian (finally!), Olivia Newton-John and hundreds more listed in my book. I'm still to meet Avril Lavigne who, to this day, is my modern music role model.

When asked what kind of books I like to read, I almost without hesitation reply opt for music biographies. I love to read artists detailing moments and events behind the scenes. I love the journey and the excitement that these take you on. I think the best music biography I read was *Scarred* by Jerry Dammers of The Specials and Alex James's *A Bit of a Blur*. Not to mention *Dancing with Myself* by Billy Idol and *Anger is an Energy: My Life Uncensored* by John Lydon. I think it was my quest to be a musician and my psychic ability that I was drawn close into a circle where I was allowed to get close, see, speak and write of meeting some of the biggest names in rock, pop, modelling and TV.

Jenna Jameson's book, *How to Make Love like a Porn Star*, was as influential to me as it included the look and detail I aspired. She was such an influence in my teens, I loved the extremes of all American glam blonde. The pornography were her steps and codes if you read her well. I was also influenced by Brigitte Bardot, who played a crucial figure in how I wanted to look.

I am strong yet still childlike though I have survived and named myself the DESERTblonde, the strong one. So get yourself ready for the modern day Rock 'n' Roll Porn and Psychic scandal you may ever read. I put my all into this book and worried about the consequences. If it were anything less, it would beat the reason why *In Stitches* is best seen complete.

You'll see here how someone, who aimed at music stardom and someone found a relation to the life of Jenna Jameson - her struggle to reach the bar and see her fall down. There is no middle ground description or recognition in the careers of musicians or porn stars who breathe each day to be something, yet have to take side roads to get there. There is a belief that fuels people like this and I know my life has been about surviving massive hurdles and lows to gain feet to get to where I always thought I belonged. The CODES I designed to keep going are individual stitches with a hope it will someday be enough as it's all I know.

TIMELINE

1969: I was born Jolyon Winston-Bray on January 31st, 1969 in McDonald Road, Lightwater, Surrey, UK.

1969 — 1978: In my infant years, my family moved a lot including a home near to Windlesham, Surrey, UK.

Following that, we left for a newly made Spanish hill villa for two months in Girona-Lloret.

Afterwards, finally left Europe for Rio to live for seven years where I attend two schools.

My mother had many dinner parties with government dignitaries and friends such as Michael Heseltine

1979: Returned to UK and attended my third or fourth junior school in Reading, UK, for less than a term, and then moved schools to start at Woodley Primary outside the city.

1979 — 1980: We moved from Winnersh in Reading to Burnham to live with my Grandfather at his home called 'Silver Birches' in Burnham Berkshire to my final junior school, St. Peter's Middle School.

1981: I moved up to Burnham Secondary School and the beginning of pain and bullying rears its first head. Music lessons with teacher Mr. Mazurion were my only respite.

September 1982 — July 1985: Left Burnham for Windsor and attended Windsor Boys School, Berkshire, UK. I wished attended Eton or, even better, St. Mary's Convent in Ascot, Berkshire. We moved in my Aunt Sandra's home with my cousin Sallie, together in Windsor at Athlone Square, Ward Royal Windsor. Windsor Boys School and my new tormentors came at warp speed, fights ensued and even my favoured art class was only a slightly temporary rest place.

1986: My band Lonely Crystal Child played our first and only gig before I left for LA in April 1987. On April 21st, 1987, I met one of my ultimate heroes Olivia Newton-John at her store Koala Blue, in Melrose Ave, Los Angeles, CA.

1987: Two local girls Anne and Suzy Nealson who attended the Windsor Brigidine Convent School sang backup in my first solo record and live performances. Eton band Thousand Yard Stare were my support band. Playing at noon, it managed to allow all the girls from many schools to attend.

1988: I moved to Bath, UK, to live with my then girlfriend Anne Shenton (my Cousin Sallie's best friend from school). Years later Anne formed electronic outfit art band Add-N-X, who signed to Mute Records. I hated Bath and so dyed and shaved my hair to assume Gary Numan uniform all over again. My anarchy against all these slightly effected students into The Smiths and pretending they're all poor, and depressed listening to Joy Division. I was very lonely here and Anne was mostly happy here, yet we were distant. Finding out later she was cheating on me with an old enemy from Windsor Boys called Paul Claydon.

1989: I started temp job #10 at The Salon' hairdressers till dreams took over and LA called again. One new stop off at The Guards Polo club before I go. Ronald Ferguson stormed around the club in his beaten up old red BMW and I later assisted him out of a pickle with the press. I was never sure if he even realised, or did he?

1990: Polo, Polo, Polo!

1990 — 1995: Band Republica's founder members, who were my old mates from Windsor go off to reign supreme in the UK and tour the US. In between the mayhem I arrived at Holland Park tube and met up with their guitarist Johnny Male. The Soul Family Sensation was his band until he asked his then girlfriend Anne Shenton 'Are you (Ready to go)?' T-shirt wearing indie Johnny, with clenched beer to his chest, enjoyed his star rise in the charts in the UK and USA. Some dreams happen. Meanwhile, I am beaten, worn and recording music of the future again at other star studios as you did back then.

1998: Edna my late Nan answered my question six months of who would be my next girlfriend. An artist, she proclaimed. In he walks and my latest song, Nebula Blue, three weeks later gets its somewhat odd airing in-front of 52 million viewers on the Gong Show at the Sony Lot in Los Angeles.

1999: (Hell- Hengelo' Holland) New Year's destination by train with Michelle and friend Christina to celebrate with Arjen Hartman, who I made friends with, back at Jim's 'At The Beach' hostel on Venice Beach, CA.

2000: I finally moved away from the scene and The Strokes are the New Order on the playlist of every radio station in the UK. Holland Park in Kensington became my new home and Michelle moves in.

2001: I acquire an agent by default. I impress, yet upset, Celebrity Columnist RAV from *News of the World* paper. My automatic psychic reading sealed and signed which I hand to my agent David, turns out to be 'too accurate for him' to believe. Next stop was the offices of *Marie Claire* magazine for interview and photo shoot to tell editor she won't be here long.

2002: Move to heal friend and roomie Bananarama singer Siobhan Fahey. I record my next album, Sensyon Approaching, in her garden recording studio.

2003 — 2004: Many gigs and solo shows performed and my beloved car dies on route home from celebrity wedding in Lewis, Brighton of Richard Norris, of famed 90's dance band The Grid.

2005: Went to LA for a trip and landed home to an email from my editor Mary Bryce of *It's Fate* magazine following my *Marie Claire* celebrity predictions. I'm offered my own column and almost missed a very important email when Mary asked if I'd consider auditioning to be the resident psychic on Big Brother's Little Brother TV show in the UK. Followed this was the recording of my own track for the label, God Made Me Hardcore, along with Siobhan, by producers Andi Chatterley and Richard Norris.

2006: More TV offers and appearances on UK shows were offered to me, such as Channel 5's Unanimous fronted by comedian and presenter Paddy McGuiness whom later found true success hosting dating show Take Me Out.

This year also saw me sitting with Michael Jackson in his car backstage at The World Music Awards in London. His hands felt rough and if only I could have been left with him alone I could have helped and warned him about things. In this year I visited my GP to ask for help in my soul desire to become a woman.

2008 — 2012: Start of many, many operations and, of course, my initial full GRS op.

2011 — 2012: Opportunities aplenty came from Adult World, Psychic Today TV, Loaded TV, Redlight-Playboy TV and ChatGirl TV.

2013 — 2014: I joined City Warrior Boxing. My trainer Gary Stasek led me to the ring until 2016. I meet Mathilde, a property design mogul and was appointed her assistant.

Both were a guiding light to one another. Her lasting remark to me, "I met you one year ago where you were so broken you could hardly form sentences. Now you are stronger and focused, but still a bit wild."

2015 - February 15th, 2016: Pinewood Studios are going to tell my story of the last 40 years as I try to heal from all my stitches.

May — July 2016: Music somehow becomes my saint and I put together a new studio to create and compose. Had been working on some orchestral themes with a working title "Errās", then decide to write some new rock n punk songs. This Rebel Still Runs.

In Stitches

Chapter 1 — Lonely Crystal Child

I was born with the name of Jolyon Winston-Bray on January 31st, 1969 at 2am, in McDonald Road, Lightwater in Surrey, England. My mother Wendy, a former debutant to her own former years in Ascot, Berkshire. My father was gone from our lives when I was only four after committing adultery. It would be years later I was told of his infidelity and met him only once in my teens. I attended Windlesham Infant School though I have no clear memory of this, as I went in total to nine schools by the age of sixteen.

Spain, or more specifically, beautiful Girona-Lloret is really where this journey must begin. My brother Giles, mum's then partner Herbie and I arrived in our hill side house which was only just completed. It was so new in fact, I can vividly remember the smell of fresh white paint. We slept in a row in sleeping bags and I played with my black and gold JPS racing car on the bare floor for entertainment. We spent only two month here, enjoying the hill side walk down to share the village pool and hear sounds of crickets and castanets.

Herbie was like a new dad, though I was too young to give him an interrogation. Who are you and where did you meet mum? He seemed a rather hidden and quiet man, seemingly distracted by something and was slightly strict. Our stay here in Spain was only for two months for reasons

I'm unsure. Soon the next destination was about to be revealed. Herbie worked for FARANTE an electronics company based near Bracknell in Berkshire, England.

My birth father John Winston-Wigglesworth absconded before I even got to draw conclusions or images. Though I recall a shocked sound as my mum answered the door to him when I was sixteen. Later I was told he had asked a distant relation about where mum lived and asked my mum if he could see me. I believe my brother met him on a separate occasion in a nearby pub. I suppose I was quite reserved and distant, only questioning if that was his yellow Citroen outside. He owned a car showroom in Ascot near where my mother spent her younger years. I never saw him again and I was told it was my choice if I wanted to see him again. I had no connection emotionally by 1985 and don't think I really thought much past this. I had been through so much by the age of sixteen and went through by myself.

Herbie was set to be relocated to Rio so the family rolled up our sleeping bags and set off to an even hotter climate.

Chapter 2 — Brazilian Algebra

Arriving in the mid-70s to our second floor apartment 694 Visconge de Abacourkee road in Leblon, the heat was incredible. It took two weeks to accustom ourselves, Copacabana beach reached as far as my eyes could tell. The sand a mix of white and black so hot, and in the distance a man singing and drumming a chrome canister strapped to himself. We drank cold tea which was great relief in the heat. Volleyball was played everywhere and we loved it. Giles and I got our first polystyrene surfboards which we took to with great excitement.

My school was in Leblon — an Anglo-Brazilian Irish infants. It was small with hardly any air conditioning and a yard set in the middle of the school with a long wooden table, and seats where we took our lunch. In the yard a tree stood which often caterpillars sometimes dropped into your sandwich if you weren't quick enough. This was not so bad on a day when mum chose to pack our lunch box with sardine sandwiches. If they fell out from the bread, often on purpose, because of the horrid taste. Worse would come when the kids would laugh and ask "What are you eating?" For a kid like myself cursed with embarrassment this was not good, especially in-front of the prettiest blonde in the school yard. If I could have turned off the lights to the world I would.

I recall on many occasions staring out of my bedroom window somehow lost or bored looking out for some fun. The heat was at times immense and school would end by 1.30pm occasionally, so it was time to hit the surf. A Swiss blonde easily caught my eye in class and when we were allowed to pick a book to read on the stairs I went in for a kiss. Giles attended a Sunday school to advance his curriculum, six long days in education, poor him. The school system was different to the UK as years later I was to repeat a year.

Eventually, I moved up school and went to an international American school attended by kids of diplomatic parents. It was mum's turn helping to make Sloppy Joe's hotdogs for the kids, as the parents did. There were men in sharp suits and sunglasses outside the main gates. Rio was fun and we were members of Clube Navale, a hill retreat private weekend club, where I swam and Herbie pushed, keeping my head under once on purpose sending me into rage. Was this his way of teaching me underwater diving well? I was a sensitive child and I shouted to mum "Why did you let him do that?"

I feel in my heart that Giles and I tried to be close with Herbie but it was, I feel, his strict parenting style kept us distant. Though he did try, on occasion, to do something exciting like show us how to locate stars in the sky.

Happy days were trips up into the hills for weekend BBQs, picnics and mums famous vinaigrette tomato salad while hummingbirds hovered above. Once visiting Vahejuka Cristof, the symbol of Rio, mum did not want to stand at the views edge. I liked taking risks, fearless and loved the excitement. Some nights I spent walking the beach and the lights looked so pretty. I recall looking at glistening diamonds through a jewellery store. Rio's food like meats on rotation were served by your table off the skewer along with the fruit market music, beaches, football this culture — it was incredible.

The perimeter of the beachline was amazing and by day, coming off the beach to brush sand onto the mosaic pavement was like stepping onto a hot tin roof. Matching clothes seem to be a common theme for Giles and me, years later we both decided to call a day on this. Leblon was a fun area set three blocks from Copacabana beach with an exciting heartbeat and atmosphere which underlined any possibility of tension.

Fun was made by myself and my brother's antics with our red plastic cast racing peddle cars. We did side skid tricks outside the local restaurant and were offered free bread to move on. The smell of school pencils and rubbers are a fixed memory though I did not enjoy lessons and found them a chore with a sense they were not guiding me towards my future.

I lived in an apartment on the second floor of a fifty storey building with decor not dissimilar to the 1970s TV play *Abigail's Party*. Mum wore long dresses, headscarves and the largest sunglasses being DE LE GURE. We had maids and my favourite was Delfina. She was lovely, and although there were others, Delfina was part of the family. On one occasion some kids from the same tower apartments above ours played a horrid joke shouting my name from above. I looked up and as I did a white plastic bag with their excrement dropped to my head. Running while crying and angrily shouting "Mum, mum". Delfina knew how to get it out. A method of boiling Coca Cola mixed with the juice from the cactus leaf, it acted as a paint stripper. Followed afterwards by Timotei shampoo, towel and cuddles from mum. This was my first memory of what would become a childhood of bullying.

The tiles around the apartment's entry area and playground were small square and bright. These mini square tiles were still being laid one-by-one with the distinctive pleasant smell of hot tar. I recall asking the workman how he did what he did as at my young early age I seemed interested in buildings, architecture and art.

I suppose that was the bad side of this era. There were there were a few select kids who seemed to pick me out due to maybe my bright, blonde hair and English accent. It might also have been though, and only a guess, the fact Giles and I were always dressed in matching clothes. Once we wore white and blue clothes matching our bright new bikes, a beacon to the less well-off kids.

The apartment estate was made up of families from different social standings. This all added up to setting us apart from the other kids for further provocations. On a later date on the seesaw, one of the children jumped on the other side so hard, I slid hard and fell cutting my lip very badly. Later, their mothers made them come round and say sorry with faces that had seen fear from their parents many times. There was a very pretty girl in one of the apartments. She was fair and once, I kissed her and ran home spellbound.

Days turned over and sometimes I felt targeted for seemingly being different. When I could feel something was about to happen or sense other kids were wanting to pull me out I would have turned off the lights to the world to make myself invisible if I could. Why was I so different in their eyes? Was it their remarks my mother got even from when I was in the cot?

Overall our time in Rio was amazing and at one period my Nan, Edna Davies, came to visit from the UK and my brother took her shopping for her favourite scents Miss Dior and some pure cologne. *The Wombles* were huge at the time and to see them on Brazilian TV was magical. Once I remember mum waking us to say "Quick, come, the Wombles are on TV." Excited and glued, mum then turned to ask "Would you like to go and see Grandad?"

"Where, where?"

"In England," she replied.

This was almost the end of our international life. Before this, behind the scenes, something more sinister seemed to be boiling. Herbie's job and our supposed wealth brought eyes on him and, in a country in the late 70s abound by corruption, was becoming uneasy. I'm unsure whether because of the work he was doing let some men down, it was later explained after some mugged him on the street and he was dragged through the window of a moving car, warning him against his work. More than thirty years later it is not clear if his work at Ferrante in Brazil was aiding to help fight against corrupt racism or simply a mugging that was more than he could take.

On the morning after this event, mum came to our room and said "Before you go into having breakfast, don't react to how he looks. He is okay but hurt." I can recall so vividly he had his hands bound and hid his display of annoyance not being able to crack the egg shell off the top. After this event and watching another Wombles episode, it was shortly time to leave.

We left the apartment and went to stay at Copacabana Palace Hotel. It was incredible, a luxury hotel with a huge pool that Giles and I dive bombed into. By the end, a car came to escort our safe exit to the runway to a waiting plane. I remember our car between the middle of three —

shiny, small and retro in style. I don't recall arriving in Rio but I do recall leaving and being among the lucky few who watched Concorde's maiden flight arrive into the city. Before we left and the wheels of another Boeing scratch the cold tar of Heathrow, we headed for Lima in Peru.

Lima is almost somewhere that is otherling, a land filled with legend, jewels and gold found over generations. That included the Incas gold I did see. Remembering human skulls in stacks and rows in respect of those now legend. The taxis in Lima were even more precious than in Mexico or even those in New York or Cuba. Cars with huge leather beige long seats.

The altitude was so high that you are told to relax and breathe much slower to bring your heart race down. In days to follow we walk through the little village and go to the sandy steps leading to a kind of restaurant and try guinea pig. I don't know if I actually did, I rather left it to mum or Herbie to try such delicacy. Mum said Herbie wanted to visit Machu Picchu but we couldn't go. You have to go into a very high cable car and climb, a test of will and remembering mum hates heights.

So we spent time at the hotel without Herbie while his tour took him two days to see the famous sites and laid hill top like a tropical green garden. Lima is a trip of a lifetime for anyone and at that age well, mum insists it was magical although I'm sure she had some reservations. But we were still very lucky I could tell. I wondered if we were here to get off away from the men in black after Herbie. Such suspicious young minds love to wonder but as exciting as it was, like a child under duvet with first torch and radio stations so far away from the alternative. The truth may have been far less exuberant.

Finally it became time to access another connecting flight, Giles and I thought we are on route to England to see grandad and Nan, though not quite yet. From extremes of my birth will tell Surrey to Spain to Rio and Lima, our foreign adventures didn't stop then as we were bound on a connecting flight to Miami.

Was this to draw the scent off us further, or because it's a very long way from Lima to London? We stayed inside the airport for two days due to the heat outside. I do recall walking outside the airport doors once and I burnt. I don't know why we could not brave it especially as we had just come from living in Rio all those years. I believe it was the intensity of the altitude and cold of Lima that was something to do with it. Though we were only here to catch a connecting flight I assumed.

Hours were spent in the airport lounge trying to entertain ourselves. I remember mum shouted "Boys, don't go too far and stop running. You're upsetting people around." Herbie went to a vending machine and I can clearly recall the three huge sized chocolate bars for us. Like a scene from *Charlie and the Chocolate Factory* in my head they almost lit up my mind. They kept us quiet for half an hour then eventually we were told to grab our things.

Chapter 3 — New Blonde Dream

It came time to board a huge Boeing 747 bound now for England. This was it, all the years of fun surf, caterpillars, kissing girls on steps and the route to the classroom were over. My time spent in Rio and Lima has stayed forever as though later I wished we never left Rio and tried to turn it all back to no avail.

My memory turned to my school and a blonde Swedish girl at that first school in Rio. We were given access to sit on the spiral staircase to give us some kind of sense of responsibility. Though in my mind saw she was so pretty, I tried to kiss her and eventually a letter saying I was disruptive and spent time chasing girls was written. I was developing skills so young.

No more will Rio's strong fruits and yellow beetle cabs are possible, or the enchanting days out to the caves and tree park of Jardim Botanico. The trees as high as heaven and the damp atmosphere mixed with leaves and scent of the caves stay with me forever. Though now we as a family face one of our last adventures together. This plane was famous in my head for many reasons. We were, as you know, bound for England and grandad will be there waiting for us in London. On this flight, hours in, an announcement came over from the cockpit.

"Hello passengers, it saddens me to announce to you all that on this day the singer Elvis Presley has died."

I heard this as clear as a silver spoon or the diamonds in the jewellery store. But mum assures me many things happened on that flight and here's how.

It was not a steady flight and I know I used my sick bag more than once, as the plane came into terrible turbulence. I can still picture it now. The pilots decided to drop the plane a few thousand feet to get through this and there was a cocktail for fear on my mum's face I've never seen since. Once out of this stream and hurricane we climb up and carry on. Mum had a thing for Vermouth and Martini, being at the end of the seventies and being the drink of the time. I prefer to think it was the whiskey Michael Heseltine drank while attending one of the diplomatic social parties at the Rio apartment.

Looking through a tiny glare of the sliding plane window on my side I'm wearing the free headphones that come in a plastic bag behind each seat and tune into any radio frequencies. I don't know why but the discovery of the lemon zest sachet refresher was a scent I liked as I am under a spell of obscure radio stations. I don't know why but it seemed later this was the last luxury were getting before all hell lets loose in England and for years to come.

On this flight, staring out of that tiny window, I tuned between some foreign station and white noise, I came across a voice that, from that moment, I'll cherish forever — *A Little More Love* by Olivia Newton-John. I did not know of her but when I saw her picture later I was a fan and she was my first star crush. As the hours pass and I woke mum saying "Wake up, wake up. My tummy turns again, I sense danger."

You see, when we get off this plane I felt we were each alone on a new path. I thought we will need more than torches. We would need a dream, a strength, a way back out of the UK because my head couldn't take what was coming.

Chapter 4 — Aliens in the Playground

So I arrived at Heathrow in August 1977 with headlines "Elvis is dead" everywhere, but Grandad is waiting outside to greet us in his blue, metallic Maxi five door. I was eight and freezing, having come from a life in the heat traffic, tanned and blonde. When Giles and I spotted Grandad, we ran and jumped up to his huge embrace.

Everything was daringly quieter and it smelt of winter and bomb fires. The roads seemed urgent, depressed, grey, green and cold. The cold was almost too much for our bodies. Being used to the heat, it took us a few weeks to become accustomed. If I had been able at this age to see and know what was ahead, I would have said to Grandad, "I just want to hug you, but I have to go back."

Arriving towards autumn in England, and feeling like Siberia, mum brought Giles and me matching sweaters from the store *Army and Navy* for our chills. We soon moved on as we were only briefly staying at Grandad's though we would return after the next few moves near Reading, Berkshire including Flamingo Mansions. My cousin Sallie and Aunt Sandra were already living permanently with Nan and Grandad at his home, Silver Birches, in Burnham, Berkshire. I loved their house. It was a large bungalow and in less than a year Sallie and my Aunt Sandra would move to her first own home in Windsor.

Residing in the UK meant the rules of education applied, and in September 1977, Giles and I had to be put into a school. I attended a middle school near Reading, but if angels could have found me they would have discovered the most painfully distant boy in the tarmac playground.

The red, high brick walls and burnt ember winter scent were torture.

I stood in the furthest corner of this playground hating every second and I recall my teachers wondering of the reasons for my pain. They encouraged me to play the triangle in music class, yet this time I was just so mentally out of sync. Too far gone and planning my escape, up and over the red, high Pink Floyd walls. At this age something inside me knew I was going to have to design CODES, methods to survive to escape out of corners.

Soon it was Christmas and the Nativity arrived. I remember rehearsals. I hated what they asked me to wear — a white sheet with head scarf, depicting one of the wise men. I was not the flock I never would be. I think on the day of the play I wore red, white always made me feel exposed and uneasy. A star wore black and was strong, hidden, but in control. Shortly after this school nightmare, mum spotted my pain and teachers ran out of ideas. Giles was getting some home schooling, maybe this would have suited me better and my own uniform would be all black?

I was moved to Woodley near Reading, to another middle school and lost count how many I attended by this point. Reading was a horrid, huge bounding town where it seemed its residents had accepted their fate — stuck in a town of cold, dark tarmac and blue interior lit buses. I thought possibly that this new school would be better and closer to Heathrow. I don't really recall one easy day here either. Rather I was ready to hide with style but at least tried to interact.

I never really got into sport. I enjoyed watching Formula 1 in Rio and playing with my black JPS toy car. Badminton seemed to be something I took to and took command of, and was once called out of playtime to compete for a place in a competition — I lost.

Grease was out and Olivia Newton-John was hotter than ever. "Mum, can I go to see *Grease* on Saturday?" I'd ask. Now this was 1978 and Olivia was the prettiest thing I knew. I prefer you didn't know what my mum's reply was. Later I realised she thought I was too young for this movie. "I will take you to see another film with your brother called *Superman*," she later replied. Wow what a movie, I thought. I came out of the cinema onto the dark, tarmac stairs and jumped off, thinking I could fly. If Superman can and Peter Pan invented it, then why can't I?

During this Reading period, we lived in a rented house while we waited for our second readymade home to be completed. This house was an old, small home with huge mahogany drawers and big, cold beds. It seemed a strange place and we only stayed there about a week. Across the road was a slim river and an old moored boat. When Giles and I got aboard, it seemed abandoned and still. In a heartbeat a police officer appeared took us back on land, asked our names and took us home. This boat was no friend and was not going to get us to Heathrow. One evening I recall waking up at 4am freezing. The next day, mum said we're moving. It turned out that something very haunting scared mum there and we were off.

The new house was half ready and I think it was number 14 in the street. A two up two down brand new house with the smell of white paint still evident. I finally had my own room and here in secret, I could plan my escape with my red, new radio with Morse code switches and an inbuilt torch. The indicator glowed in red over the channels. Somewhere in here I could make contact with Dalfina!

The street was not finished and was more a mud road and at the end of the cul-de-sac were mounds of earth where cables and drains were tunnelling. There was also an amazing playing ground, good for any kid. I think I made friends with only one kid in the road and Giles and I were very close at this time. Another cold day whilst playing Army, I hid in a mud bunker with a stoned hilled trench and cables. I looked out for Giles and a stone came hitting, landing hard on my head, it cracked. Running again like in Rio, though this time dear Giles threw the stones. It was kids play but he seemed scared too. Mum was in panic mode holding my head in white blooded towel. Mum shouting navigations to Herbie to Reading hospital.

Twelve years of age is as explained by psychiatrists the "forming year". It is said it shapes you for the future and if so then I was surely in trouble. Painfully shy, lonely and in a strange land even though I was born here, though with no real memory. I remember when I came out of the movie *Superman*, I really almost believed I should be able to fly. Though more importantly something was happening in my head. I felt things, sensed things. I felt different and wrong in myself. Our upbringing to here was, I suppose, fairly affluent and any deep expression from myself as to the feelings were kept hidden. I think I felt I was not in the right position to say too much. Mum was fully aware I was really struggling. I was fascinated by how pretty a girl could be and I was sensing things I could not work out yet.

Chapter 5 — Chasing Lois

This new school was starting to kill me yet, art was taking my pain and on sports day I got to show how fast I'd learnt to escape. Kids appeared so interested for five minutes when I discussed about my adventures in Spain and Rio, then faces turned as though our accents suggested otherwise. I had been to Christ the Redeemer, Rio's statue of Jesus. I ate the largest chocolate bar in Miami Airport and seen Lima. So maybe the other kids thought I was telling tales, or it was too much to relate to?

I had been through so many changes in what had almost been my first little decade on earth were shaking us all, and mum's relationship with Herbie was cracking. Arguments began behind bedroom doors, some so bad I wanted to save mum. I loved to construct things and take them to school. Giles was great at constructing all manner of transportation. Waiting for him to build a plane big enough for three, though while he's learning I've made a flat spinning Lego — electric spin plate with attached paper. Placing a pen in any position and varying colour, you can create a design, after circular design. The kids thought it was amazing, though I was into science. Surely I can invent something from here?

But for the scent was intoxicating, amazing and discovering a close proximity to this aroma years later in a ladies perfume (HAPPY by Clinique). My time at this school in Woodley was soon coming to an end. Soon and no more would mum being late to pick up the last boy waiting at the school gates. Woodley Primary School produced one love called Lois whom I played Kiss &

Chase, and stood in queue to kiss. Chasing Lois was a long way away now yet she was still in my mind. Petite, bright elfin- like — so pretty is my Lois. "I'm going to Brazil do you want to come?"

I had a goldfish. He was not free either but at least I could protect him and take him to the next home soon. The *Grease* soundtrack cassette was given to me as a gift at Christmas and I loved it. Sadly mum's difficulties in her relationship with Herbie increased and even though she took pride in the lawn out the back, where Giles and I flowered, you could tell mum's love for anything died.

By this point, we moved from Windlesham, Ascot to Spain. From Rio to Reading and now we're off again. Mum announced that she and Herbie were breaking up and the next day I got to put on a mini show of *Grease* for my class. They said they would miss me and I was emotional but I didn't belong. The following morning I loaded Grandad's blue maxi with the duvet, radio and my goldfish, as we said goodbye to Herbie.

Burnham in 1979 was a village split between rich and poor. We lived on the sunnier side of town close to the largest, fun peaks of adventure forest called Burnham Beeches. Giles and I shared a room again which was always cold as Grandad didn't like spending money. Although in the past, he invested a lot on his passions. He tuned his 125 against the 250cc motorbikes and won the Isle of Man Bike Trials in 1943. He later peddled a pushbike from Wales to Slough, Berkshire to eventually run and own workshops, where spirit fire components were made.

I did like Grandad's garden, however. It was cool, long and had a bricked, rocked terrace area with a small dolls house on the right. Down from the crumbling stairs to the garden that was mowed immaculately.

Following behind the lawn area was a dirt and branchy area with a bit of a trial which eventually became our own dirt bike track. This was so much fun where we could mud up our bikes. I loved to change my bike up. I had a black chopper three speed that I sprayed from scratched red to black with sticker for flames running down the side. That was the cool thing to make the bike my own. Get a frame, primmer it, spray it, put a small wheel on the back and large wheel on the front and rear mud guard raised high. I could spend a day turning my bike upside down, changing, and rebalancing but mainly mending punctures. Giles loved scrambling too and if his older friends invited me, we all raced over to Burnham Beeches woodlands.

My new school, St. Peters Middle School, was where my cousin Sallie was already attending. It wasn't long before I was being picked out by the kids and Sallie did her best to defend me though I did my best to fight back. I hated any connection with such place. All that made my heart grow fond were bikes, girls and an alien-like popstar who may have the CODES for the way out of here.

Gary Numan was a genius find. I felt so connected to him. He looked like he was from a distant place and knew he felt different too. A kid in the playground sold me Gary Numan's second album, Replica, for 50p. His band was known then as Tubeway Army before Gary adopted the name that made him famous. The man himself in all black, just like my bike. Music was complete a secret thing you could own, create, belong to — away from others.

Meanwhile, I was slowly decreasing my interest in school as the bullying intensified. Why did it follow me?

Why? Why? Maybe it was due to my pull away appearance, accent and long eye lashes or something I never quite understood. There were 365 days in a year, and I had to get my plan right and soon as each of those was hell for me. My God, it was 1980 and my only escape was music and the album Telekon by Numan which came as a live double album the following year, after his brief retirement from performing live. I loved music. The Police, Olivia, Numan and Adam and the Ants, but Gary was better. He had the CODES and I needed them.

One day, Grandad came to collect me from school as I had a bad tummy and took me in his car home. I loved him so much. His full name was William Reginald Davies and as a teen he rode his bike from Abergavenny in Wales to Slough to find work during the war. His home workshop was so exciting, with the lovely smell of damp wood and oil. He was a keen painter along with Nanny Edna, a beautiful lady with 50s style hair and strong eyes who wore Miss Dior. If Giles and I seemed lost or worried she invited us into the larder and produced each a Milky Way chocolate bar. But my anxieties started to escalate as by this point, I started to wet my bed and dreamt deep.

One of my dreams included a black magic scene in Starsky and Hutch, a hugely successful American TV series, where I was attacked from great height. Was this a psychic attack in my sleep, a night terror or just a film of how my life seemed? This scene replayed for two months until I was told when you dream, face the man, then stop, talk and see.

Eventually these frights stopped and I defeated the Macumba (Brazilian Black Magic religion). In Rio on a beach walk, Giles and I found hundreds of coins on rocks and mum shouted at us to leave them, explaining they are wishes to Gods and spirits. We got relief again from school one weekend and went to visit Sallie and Sandra at their new home in Windsor called Ward Royal (Flat 50 in Athlone Square). Sallie helped me learn the words to rock band Rainbow's song *Since You've Been Gone* to sing at the local disco where Ernie Wise came to open the hospice opposite. I think I did okay but my highlight of that night was dancing with a girl from my class for the last dance.

I drew a lot in Burnham with black marker, engraving names and logos of my favourite bands, Gary. I could draw plants and flowers from still life and learnt watercolour from lessons here and there from Grandad, and found a secret corner in the garage to maximise my creative talents.

My creative talents and my love for bike racing occasionally got me to try and impress the girls. One day, I forgot to tighten a wheel nut to produce a wheelie where I passed Sallie with her sexy best friend Jackie Hart coming down the drive. Jackie Hart's first house was on the corner of our road in Poyle Lane. She was exotic and part Italian, I think. She wore white shorts, t-shirt and pumps, she had gorgeous tanned legs. Months go by and finally, as my bravery grew, following enough day dreaming and jumping curbs (picked up from *Dukes of Hazzard*), I took the courage to ask her out. I taped a small, red and black radio to my bike listening to *Upside Down* by Diana Ross. When the day arrived, Jackie invited me to wash bikes and see her home. We drank homemade lemonade and had ice cream, almost as good and my godmother's lemon sorbet whom I stayed with one summer.

Soon after, finally, my time at Primary level was ending. I defended myself at St. Peters Primary school as well I could through music and CODES. Why do I feel alone or on my own? I see my brother each day after school who, though he is three years older, was lucky enough to have seen Gary Numan in his now famous Farewell Show at Wembley in 1981. Sadly, I couldn't go. But mum seemed very close to Giles, being her first, and that increased my adopted fear and strength.

My mum promised that after big school, that was it. I almost could tell she saw my pain but seemingly by law was powerless to stop it. It was as though she could see I had no interest in it and that I knew something, which my future had nothing to do with it. Giles always seemed to be schooled somewhere else if in Reading. I knew his time at school was difficult also. He found exams hard and the cold was worse for him. In Burnham, I don't remember seeing him but we attended my next school together for a year. He was already at Burnham Secondary when I joined.

I recall a couple of months before leaving St. Peters, we were all marched from school to see our next school and we walked down a long bramble lane to the entrance. If only I knew how badly this school was to be for me. The school was spread out — separated out buildings and a big sports hall. The kids were a mix from scattered parts of surrounding towns and areas which meant bad grapes got in. Giles didn't have a great time either and on one day, I remember standing with him while some boys made comments to him and he told me too act separate from him so he could almost protect me from them too.

I had some confidence gained in this school thanks to my music teacher Mr Mazourian. He was tall and was agitated by kids who would not pay attention, and best of all, he had drums. During one lesson, for being a good pupil in class,

I was finally allowed to choose a snare drum from his cupboard. I learnt some theory that week and was then was invited to hit the drum to the score he was teaching and he added that if I was confident mood next week I may do my rendition of The Stray Cats's *Stray Cat Strut*.

Maths however was dominated by sheer fear and fractions in room B2 upstairs in summer. Lesson after lesson the teacher tried to explain what pie unit fractions were using a chart. My mind just couldn't compute and I wanted to just go home and play Numan.

Basketball was something I could do, reminiscing the days at the American school in Rio I attended, yet the bullies were never far. February 14 came and Valentine cards were handed out by a chosen girl in class, I received barely any. This one girl with raven hair knew I liked her and, again, at the end of year disco gave me the opportunity to kiss her just the once. The bullying however became intolerable and mum knew this and plans were set.

We moved from Burnham Beeches in late 1981 to Sands Farm Drive to a smaller house with recently widower Grandad. My grandmother died the year before at Paddington St. Mary's hospital of cancer in December. I remember being in a car with her mum and Grandad going over the Chiswick fly over in London with the Christmas lights dazzling from the car windows. Edna was so frail in her hospital bed and didn't recognise me. It had only been a few small years before when Giles went with Edna to Ipanema to shop for cologne. She loved me purely and yet she was gone. Mum inherited her navy mini cooper.

Grandad seemed never to recover from his loss and drove his then metallic blue Datsun intoxicated from the local pub into the house garage, just missing my Chopper.

I loved to mow the lawn, and when he allowed me, I started up the petrol motor and moved shapes across the lawn, when the cute blonde across our way was watching.

Summers were spent riding our bikes to get raspberry slush puppy drinks or being chased by rough kids through the wrong side of town. My first job was walking Snoopy a gorgeous, lethargic basset hound owned by the Gardeners family with my mate Terry Darcy who walked an Airedale. Every Saturday morning I rode five minutes from Burnham Beeches to the home of the Gardeners. Their house was incredible. Their bathroom had a rubber based floor and a dipped bath, even modern today. They also had an indoor swimming pool in the garden where we sometimes were allowed to enjoy.

The Gardeners took Terry and me to see Grimsby vs Queens Park Rangers football match. Football wasn't 'me' so the best part of the day was eating half time pies and being driven on a Ferrari. The movie *Fame* was this year's success, it was everywhere. Yet, Terry loved the band Madness while I, Numan — we argued about that, but were quite close.

When will the smell of waxed school floors be over for me? Well, not yet. Though once I hit a full drum set at the summer school fete for the school band with bullies in attendance, breathing behind in awe at what I'd done. I walked in a year ago and I'm left the week after. I went to say goodbye to my music teacher and he said he would miss me as he genuinely appreciated my efforts. Everyone else realised I was to depart was after the school disco. I finished on a slow dance and the following morning it was announced in assembly that "We are sorry to be losing

Jolyon Winston-Bray on Friday and we wish him luck at Windsor Boys School."

I knew leaving one hellish place would give me a lift but I had problems at home too. On one vivid important day, Grandad was ailing. I sat with him and felt as though I was giving him a message from my late Nan, asking him to stop drinking. I lifted him once off the floor with my small frame and dark blonde hair with silver Numan streak. Grandad's drinking formed from his loss turned into anger with many horrible scenes behind. He seemed to alienate himself and he could make me, at times, fearful if caught messing around. He once shouted in a mood at mum about something — "And look at your son. That hair, do you want him to be a poof?" That was it, my mum was furious and things went downhill from there.

Summer came again and the kids on the street swapping 7" vinyl records as usual. I wanted my brother's copy of Blondie's *Call Me* but he wanted seven singles for one of his. I gave him ELO *Mr Blue Sky* for Status Quo, Soft Cell's *Tainted Love* or The Human League's *Don't You Want Me Baby* and Adam and the Ants' *Dog Eat Dog*. Giles took his music seriously too. He had a morning job a paper boy and rode all over Burnham, saving for a better guitar than his battered Rickenbacker.

1982 came and Windsor is a bike ride from Burnham. I listened to a lot of Pink Floyd on my rides to my new school across Eton Wick passed Eton College and over Eton Bridge round Windsor Castle, along Windsor Road to Windsor Boys School. Eton College may have been a better place for me though I fear I would have seemed a dangerous rebel. I rode from Burnham to my school each day for a few months in sun, rain and cold. It was quite a long ride at times, I'd leave the house at 7am and eventually zooming through Eton High Street reaching The House un the Bridge restaurant next to ton bridge sign, a reference to me that I was almost there.

My Grandad's increasing problems bursts to the point that an intervention was required and my mum and aunt were asking the local police station to help. Eventually, at some point, it was arranged that myself, Giles and mum would temporarily stay with Sandra and Sallie in Windsor. It was always thought we would move into somewhere for the three of us though. Windsor was now home, our stay would eventually turn into three years with myself taking the sofa.

Grandad moved into a very small, white house next to the Burnham Tuck Shop with all the soft mints and sherbet lemons you could possibly want. A stone's throw from Burnham record store where Giles bought his copy of *War of the Worlds* and I ordered Gary Numan's *Living Ornaments*, though, I could not actually afford to collect it once it arrived.

I would visit and stay weekends with Grandad at his last-but-one home and listen to the radio. *Spirits in the Material World* by The Police or Michael Jackson's *Billie Jean* playing quietly. He was lonely there yet Giles stayed more often. I loved Grandad and worried all the time if he was okay.

My fears and anger during my teens surrounding family and school resonated in my fashion choices. Clothes were such an important thing at this time and mum's leather trousers I would cut shorter to look close to MJ's look. Slightly cooler than Skin Heads or Kid Creole. Shortly afterwards I'd buy all my own clothes and they were all black, black and more black.

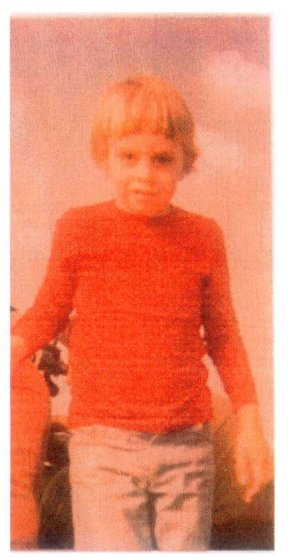

From top-left clockwise: Me as baby; Me in Spain; Me with Giles and Sallie; Nan Edna, mum, Aunt Sandra and Grandad. Mum was a debutant.

We took so many pictures of my time in Rio and Spain. Many here are of me, Giles, mum and Herbie.

Encounters with stars: Olivia Newton-John and Gary Numan

Lonely Crystal Child were a big deal in Slough.

Gigging as Sensyon in 2004 (top); and master tapes from 1993 (bottom)

Above: Me and Chessy; Below: Me in the mid-1990s.

Dreams in Flatline cover artwork, 2009. This was my 'reinvention' album.

Chapter 6 — Cold Starched Uniform

Starting another school in September of 1982 was harsh. It was as though I had to wipe any trace of my life since McDonald Road in 1969. Windsor Boys School, a recently transformed Grammar School that turned into a Comprehensive. They allowed almost any alley cat rebel and punk in. Though I was the only one with better dyed dark brown hair and a frown. I can replay my first horrid day with its Victorian, polished army floors. We were all lined up on the field and asked to get into groups according to which head teacher we were assigned. I had this nice guy for the next three years who I sensed he knew school didn't treated me well in the past.

Making 'real' friends in this school was a battle in itself. Our morning registration class had a mix of those that just missed out on Eton, and those that were on their last chance in education. I did my best to stay away from most of them and eventually found some other defunct pupils who seemingly had not travelled or been moved around a lot. They only attended big school from the middle school around the corner. I kept quiet about who I was and where I had been. Music was my biggest passion now and that's where I want to be — a real popstar and rock star.

One of my good friends there was Marlon Hughes. He was a cool looking kid with floppy feathery shiny brown hair and Bowie bleach flick that leaned over his eye. I thought this kid was someone aware of how to look silently individual. He had these chiselled cheekbones and sharp little teeth, but to a girl, he was true model material. We were both into art and these lessons were where somehow the 'cool one's' into bands segregated into factions and tribes across the room.

Late 1982, and Duran Duran is fighting Wham to top the charts. I was a fan of their guitarist, Nick Rhodes who looked so interestingly cool. Nick wore make up and pixy boots and wide over flapping jackets with draped ropes. This was also a time of the skin heads and John Lydon's second punk funk incarnation PiL which my troubled class mate and I loved. The kids in art were divided and Marlon was no servant of the peace. He either made noise or beat whoever called him a floppy poof.

From Ascot, Berkshire and his brother Paul a year up from us, Marlon was raised by his cool, free hippy mum and dad. His father was a lovely man — a Bob Dylan lookalike it seemed. They were such an open family, smoking something, Marley booming from speakers. One Saturday, he showed me how to tune a guitar. Yes that's it, Marlon's 'in'. His house though was just up the road from my birth father's garage. Tribes in music have been in that area ever since Elvis became a sensation.

But art class was just great. While some kids had no interest in music, lessons here was where the cool drew replicate album covers of their favourite band. I was a futurist, not a punk, casual or new romantic. I loved Numan and Japan. Marlon was laid back, cool and also mad on them. Hours were spent hanging, playing guitars, though not well, and listening to Japan's *Oil on Canvas* live 1982 double vinyl LP.

Despite this friendship I had, I was aged 12 and yet felt such deep despondency. I had these feelings close enough, in my own mind to view but deep enough to hide, and deep they must go while at my final school. This school was just a long stone's throw from Eton, but I'd have needed a row boat to just leap across the Thames stretch, keeping our schools even more worlds apart. Windsor Boys had this almost prepared grace that it was more than a transformed Grammar school. It was ready to take on any rough child, but interested enough to spot any genius lurking. But, I just wanted this period of my life just to end.

I was at this school for another three years and I was soon though to learn how strong my deepened feelings were. I was also a year away from finding out I had a lifelong ability. Adding to this, for all the comments and fights and taunts in and out of class, one thing I knew was I wasn't gay. But why did some kids think so? At 14 we are all fighting for our corner girls and school desk, but I wanted out. I really didn't care. I think I gave a kind of instinctive knowledge to my teachers that I've already done this long enough.

I just felt strongly again that school was not going to have any connection with what I want. I learnt to build more CODES as, and on top of all my school pain, I wasn't comfortable with the way I looked. I hated my teeth for a start, protruding with some upper milk teeth still intact and I had horrible issues with the gaps. I wanted longer hair, much longer hair, and discovering concealer was like a magic stick to temporary perfection. I wanted to enter the gates as though I looked like a star. Different. Polished. Beautiful.

And even my clothes were getting increasingly blacker. Bands were an influence from tucker boots adopted by Duran Duran and shirts had to be right. Gary Numan's changing image was a real influence. Being a true fan, I studied his look intensely and went as far as to replicate his

1981 look from the album *Dance*. The 1930s style grey suit and trilby hat, this took guts, but when you're young, it's what you do.

Though in Windsor nothing's a go-go. Bullies and casuals' were not far away. Looking cool and remaining a true Numan-oid took bravery walking down Windsor High Street. A 14 year old boy in trilby and charity shop jacket and trousers was, for the casuals, a step to far and I was therefore a target for abuse. Weekends were usually spent hanging alone, and walking the bridge from Ward Royal flats was a walk towards self-torture for me.

To add to my new pain, mum announced we were staying here in Windsor, and Grandad's wellbeing was my worry. I remained on the sofa whilst Giles on the floor. It was a short walk from Ward Royal to Windsor Boys and entering the gates, I wished the red phone box that stood there could beam me away. I did my best as a pretty faced brown dyed hair boy to look 'hard', though my moody bee stung lips were not enough.

As the months drew forward and news cameras reported that my Grandad passed away and this broke me. I don't think it was because of booze he died though, but of a broken heart. I felt that I need to communicate with him now and tell him l love him and I'm wasn't happy either. His funeral was attended by many at the Stoke Poges cemetery near Slough, Berkshire. I remember getting into the car to the funeral with everyone silent. I was keeping my love and tears silent too. Arriving I remember trying as I could to appear cool and unaffected. As the coffin went in and the curtains drew, I cried my poor little heart out. The wake was okay and peter who was a relative, drove Giles, Sallie and I home speeding with *Pretty in Pink* by

The Psychedelic Furs playing loud, in an attempt to raise our hearts.

I found Grandad's loss too much to bear as though I wish I could have done something different. I was thinking of him in his final old people's home behind the rusty corrugated bunker style workshop he owned so many years before. "Mum can we go back to Rio," I said, "I'm afraid not. Be brave. Your grandfather would want you to be like this." By this time, near 1983, I had probably seen more, been through more, attended more schools and had more experiences than anyone in registration the next week.

I didn't know why but school was starting to hurt and the bullies were starting to pick me out, maybe for my disconnection in the huge playgrounds or classrooms. By this time I knew what I wanted to be in life and music was the answer. Two boys started to be an annoyance calling me an alien or poof, queer or gender bender. I had no understanding why. Was it my hair, lips, neat look, as I wasn't remotely gay? I was chasing girls as though they were a top going out of fashion and gorgeous. One girl I was fond of was named Stripy because we lived on stripy leggings. With her wild, natural, dark, curly hair, she was my new muse. She was attending Windsor Girls School, we chatted and kissed in zero degrees cold until I walked her home.

One weekend in WH Smith, wearing my Gary Numan Tour t-shirt, I notice a skinny, white, haired boy looking just like Gary. He strode up to me and said "Are you looking for the Numan section?" Yeah, I replied. He introduced himself as Richard. We talked and talked all excited that we met another fan. Making me feel a little more attached and less lost I followed him round while he served other customers. We agreed to hang and next weekend I was invited to his house in Dawley Ride, Colnbrook, close to the Punch Bowl pub. His house was in a bright row of 70s properties.

Brenda, Richard's mother was a lovely lady. He was once of three brothers and had one sister. All were very different yet all very quiet, and his father Norman always seemed interested in what we were doing. Though I sensed early Richard was the black sheep and had difficulty communicating with him well. Richard's room was covered every inch in Numan posters and he even painted his windows black and had wooden, red painted strips of wood as Numan's *Telekon* album from 1980. The windows cracked through the heat of the sun but even more magical was that he had a synth. The first time I'd seen a synthesiser was months previous while racing along with Marlon and gang on our bikes to see a 'Wasp' synthesiser — black and yellow from the music store on Eton High Street opposite the river bridge from Windsor Castle.

When I was fifteen, my senses were rising so much, I started to see images of another person in the future. I was feeling and seeing full film clip type imagery in my mind. I felt pulled, almost like someone can hear me, and all my thoughts from afar. I hated the way I looked at times. I asked Grandad once "Can you tell girls are so pretty. Why could I have not been one?" The thoughts were increasing more by the month and realised I've been having these since I was twelve.

Back at Richard's, he begin to play including a version of *Down in the Park* by Gary. I was so excited, the sound was amazing. He announced we could play together but I was going to need to sing. I had a voice, having taught myself techniques through listening to Olivia Newton-John and Michael Jackson. Over the following weeks we practiced and when we stopped for a break, his mother knocked on the door asking if we wanted sandwiches, and apple crumble — how nice.

Eventually we started practice a song Richard wrote and spent hours rehearsing. We thought by this time we could be a band and wondered what to call it. Writing ideas on scrap paper then throwing it away and so on. Then I thought back at my days at school where by the second year, it became insufferable, hiding, fighting, avoiding and even bargaining with Mathew Marsden and Mark Curlew who were my main opponents. I felt lonely though determined to survive. I came up with a name for the band and told Richard, "What do you think of 'Lonely Crystal Child'?" It was settled upon and both of us were happy and furthermore, I knew how deep the name went. 'Lonely' at school and more 'Crystal' in reference that I will come through and 'Child' as I felt.

I hated school and for some reason, I had no interest in history. I was a futurist, so the past and old, ruins and events didn't remotely connect with me. Drum lessons were a big yes and my mother, now working at a local fashion store, offered me to have them with Alan Roberts. Opposite the school was a church and upstairs a practise room where I was taught. The huge thud of the tom-toms and kick drum got me excited and I walked up. Alan played a loud solo then stopped to introduce himself. Following this he explained about the lessons, duration, days and it was settled, mum sorted payment. Finally he said "Next week, bring in a 7" single you want to play to, and I'll teach you."

I took in The Police's *Message in a Bottle*. I went for a year I think then, as my main exams were coming, I faded a bit though I had by this point pretty much learnt how to play. Also I taught myself how to twiddle and rotate the drum stick many times which would serve me well in order to impress a girl.

Soon, I extended my musical interests to picking up the guitar and playing soundtrack to David Sylvian's 1986 masterpiece *Gone to Earth*. Finally, a bass guitar was asked upon for our band practice, though it was pretty soon realised at that time, a Roland Bassline effects box would do better. I was withdrawing from lessons and couldn't stand going there anymore. Marlon was off leading his followers dressed in his baggy trousers and black jumper, and in-turned white collar with black tie worn outside. He did fashion well and manoeuvred around school dress code well, preferring to dress like his hero David Sylvian.

The second year seemed to take forever and I frequently tried to avoid lessons pretending I was sent to another class or lost whilst all the other kids were in class. Eventually the head teacher asked me to wait behind after morning registration and said there is a man who would like to meet you, go with this boy. I dealt with so much up to this point in all my schools and avoided with grace things no kid should have to go through. I sat in this room and this man asked me how things were here and at home, then produced subliminal pictures and asked me what I saw or felt by each image of odd ink blots and random shapes used in cognitive therapy.

I was sent to see a child psychologist! I was so annoyed and stated "I don't have a problem, they do," and walked out. Later it turned out that mother had been called many times up to the school without my knowledge and asked "Don't you know your son is on drugs?" I had not touched or even seen drugs. The closest I came was Marlon's dad smoking a spliff. I further started to distance myself from everyone, shielding myself from teachers in books and falling asleep as dribble fell in an attempt to escape.

Things became so serious I was truly exhausted and beyond anger, lacking energy to live. Summer of 84 came and my mother was seeing a man who was in the RAF in Cornwall. She took me that summer to get away from the longest term ever. I ran on the beach and rode one of his bikes with my headphones singing along to band ABC's *Lexicon of Love* in my ears. I watched Duran Duran Rio tour on his television in a world of my own while mum seemed worried. She did care when she pulled me out of schools in Woodley, Reading and Burnham Secondary.

When I started my fifth year of secondary school I knew this was my last year ever and I would never ever, after this, go near an education facility again. I tried so hard in this new term and even impressed my new Head of Year with my artwork, gaining our year an award and I wrote well in English. Though, I sadly had to prove I wrote this piece. I knew I could write yet not spell well with bad punctuation, but I had vast ideas. Richard and I were adamant of being better and practiced harder and harder more sandwiches 'Big Mumma' as I called Brenda. She was not big, but her heart was and I felt relaxed and as I was doing work I loved. This was the only thing I looked forward to each week. Richard attended a different school which a young Gary Anthony James Webb (GN) had also been to, so Richard tried to find any reminisce of Gary's work.

Band practice was truly now the only thing I looked forward to and I had a friend on my side into the same music, looked cool and different as Bowie was. We sometimes went on very long walks talking about music, and met up on Saturdays to hang and talk music or girls or about Gary's latest album or more.

Aged 15 was when I started psychically seeing things and could stare at someone and view what was destined for them. I tested and tested myself more and more until it was obvious to mum, myself and many around I was psychic. It was natural to me. I didn't ask for it. All I wanted was to be a musician.

And my musician urge escalated no end on one cold Sunday October day when my mother drove through Cobham in Surrey and announced "That's where, I believe, Gary keeps his plane." Mum turned into the aerodrome and parked up by the grass. I looked around from the window. After about ten minutes or so, in silent shock, "Mum, mum, look. There he is." I recognised him from miles away. The back of his head, black dyed hair and flight baseball cap. "That's him," I proclaimed.

I got out of the car and grabbed one of his singles I had spread across the back of mum's car window. *Are Friends Electric?* was the one I chose. I noticed Gary talking with another pilot so I waited. Eventually I walked up to another pilot and said nervously, "Can I say hello to Gary?" He said it must be odd when your favourite star is standing feet away, wait here. Gary then came up to me. I was so nervous I could hardly talk yet Gary, even with his Asperger's kept up the conversation and signed my record, and told me about his upcoming tour. I smiled and went over and over it all on the way home. I rang Richard's house to say "I've met him," yet he was out so told Brenda Mills all the details.

"Oh how exciting," she replied. "Richard will be excited and would want to know. I'll get him to call."

As final exams drew closer, I concentrated on my O-Level art and drew, scrapped for final submission. A long, hot term came went until signing off day. The week before I told my careers officer I was going to be a popstar and he said "I'm not sure we have any vacancies! Though maybe a job at the local menswear shop would be better."

On my last day, I walked around all my teachers knowing I completed all my exams and of the legal age where I could tell them where to go. I walked from class to class and collected all the teacher release signatures. I remember my form teacher who stood up as I interrupted his classes he well knew what I was doing there. He exercised his wealth of having taught hundreds of boys' year-by-year. I knew he spotted I was in trouble and alone from the set.

From all those years from Spain to Rio, to Reading, to Burnham and Windsor. No more will this go on. I'm so truly done. You hurt me forever, but I'll decide to find a way to survive my future. Though I later came to peace in myself. Although I would never forgive, I would try to forget one day for myself. I ripped up my leaving papers as I reached the school gate, and walked out with an enormous sense of relief, fear and excitement about being a musician and visiting LA. Though once I walked the ten minute walk to my home, I felt used, older, numb and alone.

Chapter 7 — LA Calling

The months preceding me leaving school, I was sure I did not want to go to further education. I was gladly done. Now I had to set on a plan. My school exam results arrived and I achieved five CSE grades including in English, Humanities and Maths, and a grade D in O-Level Art. I was also slightly colour blind as diagnosed at Woodley Middle School in Reading. As it was explained then I would not be able to do one of my dream job as a pilot, or a policeman which was not my intention to become anyway. Here I was, sixteen years old, exhausted, and now all I wanted was to be out of the UK and a musician.

I needed to save up for leaving Britain. So I walked around Windsor, applying for jobs here, there everywhere but with no interest. Weeks would go by and in September I was accepted onto a hairdressing apprenticeship at Ritz's on St. Leonards Road, Windsor in Berkshire, England. I began my post at the hairdressers, learning, sweeping and taking calls, though months later I was daydreaming and was just looking for my escape which distracted me from fulfilling my role.

In June of 1986 mum, Sallie, Sandra and I went to Rhodes in Greece for a holiday and I managed to wash away the last six months, and listened to music whilst attempting to gain a nice tan. I met a girl at our hotel who took a shine to me. She was blonde, petite from north England and had a week left on holiday. We spoke and one evening met at the hotel disco and kissed. Though never far from bullies, some Greek kids made gestures at me and eventually came over to try assuming to her I was gay because I wore a small circular earring in my right, not left ear. This made you gay in their eyes. I wore my tiny earring this side as it was exactly where Gary Numan wore his and he wasn't gay either. It didn't make it any easier for me due to the fact that I was from the UK, had a pretty face and dyed black hair.

Later that week, my romance was short lived as I got caught by her with a German girl in the lobby and she saw me. The up points were lounging on the beach and to my complete thrill hearing *Change Your Mind* by Bill Sharpe and Gary Numan. I ran around as if I wanted all the sun bathers to realise it was Numan. I sang, sang, and sang.

On the last evening I remember at dinner, as though it was planned, mum asked me what I was going to do now as I left my job. Mum was a single mother working very hard at a ladies fashion boutique in Windsor. I sighed as I felt cornered and I replied, "I'm going to do music." She seemed worried and Sandra directed her tone of disapproval as well adding, "But can you play?" All the pressures of my life seemed to come and scare me.

Home in the late summer, I was lethargic and could not motivate myself to do much, yet I did spend a good week typing on an old ink typewriter, song lyrics and created a portfolio. I posted my demos to a London music publishing company that looked after Adam Ant and the like. I had a small battle on my hands here as that company were caught using my work and I fought to get all of it back. I won that battle eventually, but it helped me realise that I must be good enough to be published then.

The remainder of this year I went from job to job and mum was getting more and more worried, yet I was active in chasing my dream to be a musician. Richard and I decided to hire Neil as our band photographer. He became our third member to my annoyance. I did like Neil but Richard had not consulted me about him initially. We had been helped by Richard's father to get a day's professional recording session at the local Padded Cell recording studio, based in an industrial area close to Richard's home.

We recorded *Loves Cold Frame* — I was on vocals. I suggested to Richard we need to go live yet I sensed his nerves in this area, though I was born to perform. We did do our first and only official gig not before another cancelled due to Richard charging for a charity gig. Maybe he was being cheeky or thinking ahead in a cut throat industry. Or perhaps he needed the money for a new effects pedal?

When our first gig did go ahead, at Slough Town Football Club on November 8th, 1986 for the local Observer Mobile Screening Appeal. Our gig was part of Battle of the Bands contest — how cool — and we were the only electronic synth rock band and seem to attract groupies. After that successful gig, all of us went to Regals Nightclub in Uxbridge and the DJ announced, "Lonely Crystal Child are in the house." I think we came second in the contest and were on cloud nine feeling like teen rock stars. We worked so hard to get here and I felt like I was doing what I truly loved.

April 21st, 1987 was a date I can never forget as you will discover. When I had nothing to do I would travel into Windsor and see mum at 96 fashion store, her second job at a fashion store. I loved to hang around and mum suggested I read the ladies, advising them on outfit choices, colours and lines which I had a knack of. On a sofa at 96 I read for these women and started to grow a reputation —

my client list grew. Somehow, and I don't know why, but by staring at a person's signature and rotating it right, I could mark out with a pen through the signature events, dates, times initials that of references to their past, present and future. This was so unique, I put a small ad in a local paper as a psychic and started to read from home.

Mum by this point met a new man called Tony, a Jewish rag tradesman from London. She started to stay with him in Osterley, West London more and more. This meant that a lot of the times, I would live with just Sandra in the house, and I had opportunities to play some of my favourite VHS's but I knew by this point, my relationship with my mother would begin to disintegrate. Grandad left a will which he left each his grandchildren £1,500 which I'd spend on days out and Numan clothes.

I knew I was drifting away from my mother on one March day in 1987 when we went on another Sunday drive and stumbled across an antiques fair — something she actively goes to across the country. She often raised her annoyance whenever I wore my red and black Numan jacket, which I happened to have donned it that day. She said I was not to embarrass her and this turned into an almighty horrible scene. I stayed true though our distance and my further retreats seemed to have left us silent.

Though on this Sunday I said, "Mum, I'm going to Los Angeles soon."

"What do you mean?"

"I want to go to LA and I will."

As weeks goes by I was adamant that I would see what LA had for me and if it will accept me. Once mum noticed I meant it and researched flight prices, she told me you were not meant to get your inheritance until you are twenty one, but I will let you have some. That was it, I was going. My flight was booked with no hotel though at Heathrow Airport, my mum produced an envelope which had details of a hotel she booked me into for two weeks. All those terrible years at school, this time I'm free. Walking to the gate number for my flight I was scared yet excited. Mum was crying so much, we hugged. I told her not to worry — I have done all I could here and I wanted to go.

I arrived at LAX airport excited, but not sure at how to find out information. After three years with my band I had enough of the egos typical of most first bands so left and went solo. Reflecting back at the airport there was no need to be nervous. I was fearless and had done my part of the deal.

My psychic skills had developed by this point and I heard something to my left ear my name. It was repeated to my left ear, "Joly, Joly." Oh my God, I recognised the voice straight away. It was that of Enda. Her voice loud and so clear, so running to my visiting mum in tears. "Mum, I think I'm going mad," I explained, and she raised a smile. She asked me to come in to the sitting room to explain something. Many years before, she visited a renowned medium who forecasted that I would have the 'gift' and travel.

When I first moved to LA, I lived Santa Monica and the Carmel Hotel on 1st street (frequented by many escorts, I later found out). I passed customs and arriving to the terminal exit doors to the sweet smell which I later discovered was smog. I didn't mind — I was in LA. Before I was taken to Santa Monica, the minibus driver dropped a few other travellers which was a thrill getting to see all the different areas. Roads and highways, and lots and lots of palm trees until the next drop off was mine, opposite the Santa Monica hostel near the porn cinema.

I was nervous, alone, excited. A young seventeen in the land of angels and tattoos. I belonged already. I stepped out from the hotel doors onto the street hiding my fears and shock from the sudden heat. Following the people across the street I walked less than a block to the boardwalk and round the front of McDonalds over the road passed the Civic Centre theatre where Numan performed in 1980.

I settled in LA very quickly and visited Santa Monica beach and notice two very pretty girls. From somewhere I summoned bravery to introduce myself and straight away a platinum blonde in red bikini says, "Hey, you're British." She introduced herself as Crystal and her friend Shannon. "Hi, lovely to meet you I'm Jolyon."

Crystal was very pretty, milk skinned rock chick and sixteen. She drove an old beaten black Dastan and Shannon was a gorgeous, mixed race girl — both so kind and fun as we swap stories and questions. Crystal seemed concerned I was alone and suggests I visit her and her mother in Alhambra. The following day her mother calls me at the hotel and with her soft spoken voice says "I will pick you up on First Street at 5.15 after I finish work." She worked for a law firm. Automatically she made me feel comfortable and says "You will stay with us tonight and have dinner. Crystal is looking forward to seeing you."

We drove for about an hour and I was happy as we cruise the 10 freeway to the 310 to Alhambra, a mainly oriental suburb not far from Pasadena. We arrived and Crystal was all smiles and her mum started dinner we relaxed drinking from a white plastic drinking beaker with Koala Blue

64

emblazoned which I recognised from Olivia Newton-John's store.

Crystal and I became close and drove us all over the back of LA, maybe by routine we dropped into a fast food Drive-Thru on route to more LA fun. A day or so later, back at my hotel, I asked the front desk if he knew how I could get to Melrose Avenue (home of Olivia's store). He drew me a map plan and wrote bus numbers explaining the LA road grid system. I was told to ask for a 'transfer' which the driver handed you, from his usual tanned driving gloves. A transfer allowed me to cross grid to my destination on another bus.

Getting off on Pico and Vine, I waited for the next one to Melrose a few blocks down from Sunset Boulevard. Years before River Phoenix died at the Viper Room owned by Johnny Depp close by. Eventually I found Olivia's store Koala Blue. I was like a boy dazed. This shop was bright, selling fashion goods with a health bar. I bought a jumper emblazed with KB on and some other bits. I sat up at the bar area and asked the guy "Have you met Olivia?"

"Oh yeah."

I had a list of questions. Until he said "Why don't you ask her for yourself?"

I turned and froze as there she was. I was in shock. The women whose voice echoed in my ears on that ill-fated flight from Miami to London. I could not speak, but begged the guy behind the bar to introduce me. Olivia came up to me. I could hardly speak, her incredible eyes. I told her I had been a fan since 1978. She seemed happy and after signing her name on a fresh piece of paper. I asked her sister Rhona if she minded taking a photo of Olivia and me on my mini camera. On the final snap I planted an anxious

65

kiss on her cheek. She smiled and then Olivia introduced me to her husband Matt Lattanzi whom she met on set for the video single *Xanadu*. He was a tall guy with amazing, deep eyes and spoke to me while Olivia tried on clothes. Then, by my glee and accident, Rhona pulled the curtain when Olivia was trying clothes. I saw her in her red knickers — amazing.

On leaving, I was on cloud nine. I turned back one last time and saw Olivia and Matt looking back smiling. My God, I've come all the way from England and met Olivia. I was dazed and walked miles back through the streets on route home. Stopping to rest, I asked this old guy cutting his lawn directions. I recognised him as actor Ed Asner a normal occurrence in this city. That evening I dialled mum hearing on the pickup.

"Do you accept a collect call from the United States, sorry mum?"

"Yes, yes I do." The phone operator left the line with an "Enjoy your call" message.

"Mum, mum I've met Olivia."

"No," she replied.

"Yes, yes it was amazing," I continued carrying on explaining my adventure. Mum seemed happy in her tone that I sounded bright and not low and hurting.

A week passes and as I returned to the hotel lobby. The man behind the desk is waving the phone saying your mother is on the phone. I wondered why she wanted to call. When I answered, she asked if I was okay.

"Yeah, I'm fine."

"Do you have enough money Joly?"

My mum always worried and I suppose that was nice but I often got by and I grew fast, getting rid of some of those horrid fears from my school hood. You see, I'm with the hot blonde with a beaten up muscle car in LA and hearing some are in useless work placements, so I heard. Yeah, take that suckers.

Crystal may have been only sixteen but drove like she's got away from a few chases before. She was sweet, kind and wild and I was falling for her. I booked to go on one of the tours to see where the stars live, yet Crystal suggest I swap it and follow them to Disneyland in Orange County. I loved LA and though my short time on this first visit was coming to an end, I knew something changed in a beat for me.

When I returned from LA, Windsor seemed cold and held you back. I remember walking into where my mum worked, she was so happy to see me and cried, and her friend and boss Margaret said she's proud. The next week I walked into The Court Jester pub where all the Goths and Cyberpunks were. They in black and I in my white Koala Blue sweat shirt, though I soon went back to my own black, standard rock uniform. I could not let go of the connection LA made with me. I had to return, I found where I belonged.

It was now the dawn of 1988, I started to see my cousin's best school friend Anne Shenton. I had known her for a couple of years before we dated. She moved from her mother's only a few streets away from my old school. This shortly before she went off to university in Bath, England. We kept as close as we could and I would visit. I recall one evening where she introduced me to her friends who I believe were studying art or film. We went to see a German movie about these angels that would float from cathedrals to listen and almost point someone to the correct destination, this stayed with me forever (I believe which was remade in Hollywood as *City of Angels* starring Meg Ryan and Nicolas Cage).

I was very different to the students around the height of the bands such as The Smiths, Joy Division, and The Cure. I was a Numan-oid. I didn't connect with the student appeal and even went so far as to step into a hairdressers in Bath to ask for a Numan haircut. Then whilst the colourist went to mix colour I quickly cut and shaved my temple to assume a receded hairline identical to Gary's. Numan, I feel looking back was an adoptive father. I felt a similarity in his story and loved his singing style, voice and dark, expressive, moody, alien sound. Maybe I had to meet him again to see if he too had CODES. I feared not.

I marched into Anne's college the next day and stride to the piano and played *Are Friends Electric* with glee. I left and heard one mutter "Wow, he look just like Paul Newman." Idiots! Gary Numan again was like a force a strength when I felt scared or exposed. After what might have been my second visit I left Windsor to live with Anne though I felt so lost and wondered what I was doing there.

We argued and she was distant until I found she had been seeing a guy I knew from school. The same Paul Claydon who, at Windsor Boys, previously copied my artwork in class and now he's stealing my girl. I wanted to kill him and remember Anne writing her appeal and apology on a huge piece of white art paper. Though the next day I left Bath for Windsor deflated and mum met me at the station in Slough knowing I was worn out. She said nothing in the car though she noticed I dyed my hair dark again which to her that meant I was down.

My next step was to find work and this time I was going to help out at a Windsor hair salon name The Salon, near Eton Bridge. Two lovely ladies called Julie and Suzanne ran the business. Months later I said to Julie at lunch in the staff room, "I know you're going to have two gorgeous twin girls." A few minutes of silence passed into a very sad moment when Julie started to cry. I was mortified I'd upset my boss, though minutes passed and it was explained to me.

"I can't have children."

"Oh, I'm so sorry but I see them."

Suzanne brought me up on it later that day and said, "You must not say things like that. She's very upset but I know you can see." I met Julie a decade later in London on Church Street, Kensington with her two beautiful twin daughters. My psychic skills reached fever pitch and it's almost how I spent the next year saving to get back to LA — at least which was the dream.

I lasted about six months at The Salon as I was bored and my boss expressed with love that I was a 'free spirit' and I was quickly found work at The Royal Berkshire Polo Club. Windsor is surrounded by parkland. If you were in a helicopter looking down you would see the beautiful green fields and woods. Windsor Great Park up the hill from my house in Old Windsor is where I would next meet new lost souls to redirect.

My life was changing fast and my energy was different. I was concentrating more and more on music and recording demos. My connection with Anne was on and off yet she did, a few months later, come to the end of season party at the polo club. At the club, there a lovely lady called Hetty, an assistant to the bosses said that a gentlemen called

George would pick me up from the end of my road and bring me for my first day at the club. Another colleague, Jeff was this lovely old man who had been a goal judge and showed me around the club. He usually parked his car at Field 4. Working at the club was the only place I felt gave me freedom and time to progress as a musician and do psychic readings in the day or evening due to this being part time.

The club had its hierarchy and Jock was one. A rather moody old sergeant type who would report to Ronald Ferguson who I got on really well with. This was the end of the 1980s and the club was always in focus as Princess Diana, the princess of hearts, was often seen on Field 6 which meant Prince Charles was around. He would arrive in his Aston Martin and bolt through the gates and drive direct to play. One afternoon I was put to be ball boy and flag goalie.

But before this match, I was just sorting things and I saw a mounted horseman riding towards me and before I could think it was Prince Charles, I went completely blank. Forgetting his name entirely and before I could mutter he said "Good morning, Jolyon." "Good morning sir," I reply. Wow. Prince Charles knew my name how? The game went ahead without too many players coming of their horses, a common occurrence.

Polo to me was one of the most dangerous sports next to ice hockey or boxing. One player, King Hussein of Jordan repeatedly kept whipping his horse close to its eye, which I didn't like, but he was only doing it to engage it, maybe to work harder. At one point in the game it got too much for me to stand and I shouted, "Don't you dare hit your horse like that." He simply replied some angry excuse, yet

I was first after the game to tell Ronald of my outburst, in case I would be sacked. Though more than this, I wanted Ronald (or sir as I sometimes greeted him), to know I had animal rights at the centre of my soul. His reaction was "Well done Jolyon. These boys need to be put into place, don't worry."

I got used to seeing Prince Charles around the club and he always said 'hi'. Once, after a Saturday match that Charles played on Field 4, I asked Hetty, "How does Charles know my name?" She then explained how he remarked that I was at the club a lot and reliable. She then went on to express that Charles looked through my portfolio I left at the clubhouse with my song lyrics and photos. Hetty also told me Charles asked what I did, and then she explained I was trying to make it in music.

I enjoyed going to polo and got quite into the culture and made lots of friends. Including this one lovely couple who came almost every Saturday and sat for the entire duration watching from inside their car. Though unless to allow their two beautiful big, old Labradors to hobble and stretch. I stayed at the club for over two years more. It was a big deal to be asked to goal judge the day of the Cartier match. I was nervous but excited. With polo balls and horses missing my head at a hundred miles an hour made for great showmanship and entertainment for spectators.

I was involved heavily into the third year of recording and started to approach record companies and labels with my demos. At times, feedback was less than nothing. Though after replying to an ad in The NME music paper, I eventually heard back from a Mr Tim Autman from Paris. He said he liked my work and wished to meet with me. Mum was more worried a random man calling and suggested to Giles that he should come with me to London. "You know he has a problem with men liking him," my mum would say referring to an older man following beside me along a road home asking my name.

I was not used to this notion. I was not gay and was worn out with all the crap I had gone through in the past. I was always polite but would excuse myself, this guy expressing that I was so pretty and 'would I join him for a coffee at some point'. No sorry, I'm not interested.

I went alone to London in the end, but I arrived at Bayswater tube and walked a couple of blocks to a hotel. I sat in the greeting room waiting for him when he entered. The lighting so low against his very dark Nigerian complexion and soft accent. He said he wanted to make me into the white Michael Jackson. The meeting went well though I had been here before with labels and some dodgy offers though decided to give it a go.

This was 1989 and I rang my friend Richard Cox for advice who worked with salon owner Stewart Armotrading. He was cousin to American folk rock singer Joan, at Hack and Slash hairdressers. After the usual remarks such as "Ooh he might lock you in a room and try and have his wicked way." I dismissed them and went for it with Tim. I recall arriving at Charles De Galle airport, and felt like a real musician. I'm here because of my music, not a romantic getaway as I did in my last year with Anne.

I made my own way to Tim's tiny apartment, rang the bell almost to his own amazement that I had actually come. His reaction worried me somewhat though the following day after his wife got their daughter ready for school, I asked him "So what's the plan?" I also wanted more details such as the label we would be recording for. My questions must have been endless with the urge to satisfy my need to deem myself a real musician.

Over the following days he started to play me his music that he seemed to want me to sing. I thought that he liked my songs which he assured me, very much so, but I felt he saw voice in me to carry his blend of French Jackson-like R 'n' B. The following day we travelled out of Paris to the countryside near Lyon. After a three hour drive to his main studio we arrived at a huge decrepit barn. Behind one door he opened to reveal a massive recording studio console. Feeling nervous and slightly home sick that night, and knowing I had a thing for singer Vanessa Paradis, he produced a teen mag with her in to alleviate my fears.

The following morning, his wife prepared food, and he was making gesturing orders at her. He kept changing language from English to French. I was suspecting things but let it go. Finally we settled to begin recording and after about five takes he said, "I feel half satisfied, and I am making production suggestions about what makes a hit." He was the expert, but I feared his soul focus was to turn me into a dance act. I hated dance music. I humoured him and asked again about the record deal and contract. He then explained he had a publishing deal with Time Warner and he needed the voice to sell it.

I recall a further eight visits to Paris in one year and exhausting recording sessions. One day in the studio Tim remarked, "Your eyes, your eyes, you are so pretty. Are you sure you're not gay?"

"No I'm fucking not," I replied angrily. "Just because I have long hair doesn't make me gay."

I was not happy with the music direction and he didn't get where my music passions drove me. We hardly spoke after what became my last trip to Paris. On one trip out there, at McDonalds, he watched the amazed reaction from some French school students at my look. This satisfied his aim to try and make me into a star using only his music.

"What about my songs?"

"Yes, there's some good ones, but it's too strange for the kids."

"Rubbish. I don't want to be like every artist."

Tim felt sure I could make it referring back to our outing on the street. He said he took me out to test the reaction and everywhere we go they look. At the time, I dressed in black with sunglasses and a bit of eyeliner. The girls loved it and the guys snarled.

During my final trip I begged him for a day to myself and once agreed, I walked up the riverside and just explored. On a Sunday, I rang mum again and said "I've had enough." I felt my songs were stronger with big choruses, dance music to me was easy and not enigmatic.

I left Paris exhausted and pissed off but returned later alone for a week and stayed at a tiny hotel in Gare du Nord. I met a cool guy at the job centre to translate what the jobs board said in case I were to stay out. I asked him if he knew where Polydor Records was. I explained I wanted to drop off my demos to Vanessa Paradis label agent. He guided me and even took me for lunch at his mates — I still don't know why. He directed me to Polydor and I gave him twenty francs for his help before we parted.

Most people now send emails and post videos, but back then you really worked hard to get noticed. Create a buzz, go to McDonalds and see if the girls scream. I entered the doors of Polydor down a tiny Rue and introduced myself as a musician. I then left this envelope I had at hand to the attention of Paradis's agent.

During this same visit to Paris, I didn't really want to go home. What was I going to do in Windsor, I wondered? I mentioned to those I met during this visit that I was psychic, and started to read clients and soon realised that the messages were being translated in my mind. I was now a psychic and musician in Paris yet lonely and, eating the wrong food in my tiny room. The first time I was in Paris was with Anne. Now, I was here to get my songs to Vanessa's people. I thought what else I could do with the hope to raise enough cash and get back to LA somehow.

Regardless, I had to go back home. Each time I returned back to Windsor, I felt more trapped and lost. Again I looked for work endlessly by reading local papers, though my name as a psychic was growing and decided to place ads to some success. I had average around two to four clients a day and I was quieter at the weekends. I charged £40 a reading for as long as I could see good value. Then from almost nowhere I was aware that I could write a person's future and fill both sides of an A4 piece of paper before they arrived for the actual reading. This is commonly known as automatic writing and adding to this whilst staring at a person's general signature if rotated right, I could mark the page noting specific dates, times and names. The clients loved the latter and when arriving and sat ready for their reading I would open to them that I'd written some notes after hearing from their spirits. Their faces astounded mostly. "How do you know this?" I was often asked. I reply by going quiet and connect. My work now as a psychic medium was starting to take over and I wondered where was my music was going. No word from Polydor yet.

Stewart Armotrading, who opened the first black hair salon in Windsor, was a lovely guy and, by night, a Taekwondo master. Richard Cox was also into all manner of spiritual awareness. We had some great talks and heated discussions from music to politics until we agreed to disagree. A special occasion at Hack and Slash was when one day, a gently speaking guy looking much like Michael Jackson walked in. His name was Adrian Grant. I seemed excited. He had a presence and I would question him about what he did. He was in publishing and writing the idea for a fanzine called *Off The Wall*. A few visits later, he became more at ease around me and Stewart said "Jolyon's psychic. You should get him to read you."

Adrian said nothing. Stewart gestures go on and I stood behind Adrian sitting in the salon chair beginning to read. I say "I can see you becoming a friend of Michael's and eventually you will produce two major books on MJ then it will stop suddenly." After the reading he went to find Stewart in the tiny staffroom and said "Keep that freak away from me."

A year later I bumped into Adrian and he said, "I have something to show you." It was a picture of him with Michael in his studio at Neverland, Encino, CA. The other predictions had more of a sentiment for me due to the detail. Yet, in a period of inner pain and screaming loneliness, I sadly felt I wanted to take my own life.

Piccadilly in London a vast tourist area and I looked up at the Swiss Centre building, exploring how I was able to get in. I know I never would have tried anything, but my heart was full and broken. My view was taken by the sight of Michael's image on a book in a window with the authors name Adrian Grant., I thought I could hear in my consciousness, "Jolyon, this is what you do! You are a messenger." So I didn't go ahead with suicide.

Months go by and Stewart offers me cash to design and paint a new shop sign near home. I'm quite good at art so spend days painting in free hand. I spent so much time getting it right, by the end, Richard suggested to Stewart to give me £100 for my hard work. Julian Dale from Old Windsor was the only guy I knew around this area. He was a nice guy who I felt could almost see my soul. He was a local scooter boy and knew my brother, and a martial arts expert. Julian somehow seemed to know what pain I was in but said years later I was so strong. I think in Old Windsor I just seem to just keep myself private and concentrated on music. Girlfriends came over to mine to record or hang.

On another trip to Paris, I noticed, whilst browsing the fashion magazines on the newsstand, that Ronald Ferguson on the cover of British *Hello* magazine. Resting on white gates for his photo emblazoned on the gates that read 'The Royal Berks Polo Club'. I remember calling the club from Paris and asked if they had any jobs having previously worked at Guards' polo. I heard voices bellowing in the background.

"Jolyon, its Ronald. Where have you been?"

"Oh, I'm in Paris sir."

"Well, I need you here."

"Cool okay, I'll come home."

This period, in 1989, was a hazy and fast one. All I wanted to do was music and gain ground and success. Working by day as a psychic, and weekends at the Royal

Berks Polo Club and gigging in-between, I wasn't living the dream yet.

Windsor was a strange place for me, yet it was (and still is) the home of the Queen and whenever she is in residence, her flag goes up. But other than that, nothing exciting was going on for me. A lot of the boys I went to school with I lost contact completely by this point as I'd been away so many times. I had to get out of there and quickly.

Windsor on a good day was producing some real talent. At the back of Hack and Slash, in walked one of its luminaries, Bright New Things. Songwriter and artist Johnny Male, had indie scruff sensibility. He had such a presence and made big noises. Writing for the likes of some new chart upstarts, met with Naomi Campbell, and signed to One Little Indian record label. We became friends quite soon and anytime he was in Windsor to get his hair done by Stewart we slid down the road to the pub and chat. It always made me laugh that someone who had chart success would sit in the worst pubs in Windsor but he was a great character and made my dreams seem possible.

Giles was now living with his fiancée Stefanie and Johnny became like a brother I missed. Giles and I had been through so much after Rio after all the moves, and Johnny was someone I could talk with along with Anne Shenton, who I was still in contact with. I also was in touch with Mark Hunter who had a shop in Windsor sold all weird and strange things.

Every time Johnny was in town we all gathered at this one pub called The Prince Arthur. On one occasion this one guy came over and introduced himself as Ben who apparently attended the same school as I. I hadn't recognised him but I continued the conversation.

"What do you do now, Ben?"

"I'm an actor," he added. Later I realised he was Ben Chaplin, made famous later for playing in British costume dramas and Hollywood films). "I remember you, Jolyon. You used to wear a trilby around town and dressed like Gary Numan."

Ben asked me for a reading that day and I made him cry whilst connecting with his late mother. I told him he was going to be huge in America, which we all know he did.

Johnny was now a good friend and when his band Soul Family Sensation were near splitting, he mentioned he was going to be a solo artist but not comfortable with this, although his album Burger Habit was released with fine tracks like Los Angeles.

I found it tough in Windsor. I didn't feel I was getting anywhere. I had to go for it somehow. Eventually, I save enough money by 1992, during the dawn of Guns and Roses explosion in LA, and made my way back there. Almost five years passed and I managed to get return to LA and stayed with Crystal at her Spanish style condo in Alhambra. It had a cinema with neon elevator down the road in the distance. Nights are so hot and Richard sent me Gary's latest album on two C60 cassettes with a reflective ballad I had on repeat to think over things.

Crystal and I became close and love or sex was never quite there, though Shannon who visited from time-to-time, seemed to have a thing for me. Together we hit the streets in her car banging out GNR or hit *Baby's got Back*. One evening, Crystal and went towards a very hard-core moody rock club and pretty soon there were gestures aimed at me. The Chilly Pepper lookalikes apparently didn't take to my androgynous MJ polished look and we soon left.

As time went by, a whole new psychic experience involving the LAPD began and I started to get involved personally with Crystal who was not having a good time personally. I tried to speak, listen and advise, and to make her feel better, I offered to help her dye her from her statement platinum, explaining to go brown from platinum and instructed her to put red first or the colour won't hold. I then met Sandy Solis, this lovely Mexican — an ambulance driver for the Sierra Madre services. She lived alone with a cat across from Crystal. We seem to get on so well and invited us for beer and BBQ.

For me however, my look became more important to me and I wore makeup, powder eye liner, mascara, black clothing and my hair was long. Sandy was gay, kind, lovely and found a moment to ask whether I was gay or bisexual.

"No Sandy, I'm just a musician."

"Damn, you're the prettiest straight guy I ever met."

We laughed and I mentioned in London it was okay to look this way. She had lots of friends including another openly gay female police outrider. I was invited to a party she hosted and Sandra insisted I should attend. It ended up to be a wild party in the hills near San Gabriel and I remember kissing a hot porn star and stood on the diving board drunkenly asking if there are any girls into guys here. Having said that, this cute girl came up to me in yellow saying she wanted to have a go at having a relationship with me citing my attraction and the fact I was British.

Sandy was such a friend and invited me more into her circle. Another police officer friend was then desperate for a reading. The reading began in a normal fashion. I opened and closed my eyes, protecting myself in a blue shell of light then, invite spirit to come in. As I got further into the reading, I sensed she was working on a case at work she struggled to break. She confirmed that was the case. I then worryingly suggest, "Look, what I'm about to say is in strict confidence because I don't want the police coming to me." She said it was okay.

"What do you see," she replied.

"You know the murder case you're working on about the little girl."

"Wow, yes."

"Well, I know who killed her. There are six of you on the case right?"

"Yes."

"The guy who killed her is one of the investigators on the case. He's tall, stocky build with grey hair."

Two months passed and I received a call from her saying I was correct and she thanked me. My time in LA was almost over though from all the readings, I practically got the money I paid for the trip back. Crystal and I were getting on better and I said to her that I sensed the next time we'd see each other, one of us will be engaged.

On returning back to Windsor again, many things remained the same yet I was invited to speak by a group of friends, including Zac Goldsmith who attended Eton College, to come and speak on the subject of Psychic Phenomena in front of 900 boys at Eton School morning assembly.

On some Saturdays, a group of us made up of mates from Eton in bands, with Zac and his younger sister Jemima sat for hours on the Long Walk grass verges at the back of Windsor castle. A week before my speech, my official letter has arrived from the head Dean, my Etonian mates begged me, "Don't come dressed like us, look like you a musician."

On the day of my talk, I was greeted by the School Dean and Beak, as he was known, explaining the process of my 9am talk. My God I was nervous, though once I start it went okay. I got to the twelfth minute into my fifteen minute speech and froze for a few seconds. I felt tension as my collar microphone sound echoed across the hall. I then went to talk about a prediction I made three years ago to Adrian Grant. Adrian, by this time, made frequent trips to Neverland to see MJ in California. My talk then reached fifteen minutes and I was free. The whole school clapped and pictures were taken.

A year later, in 1993, I took my music more seriously, and I worked like mad to save as much money as I could to return to LA again. Somehow I saved enough and started to pay for the recording of my first album, *Sound for Aliens*, in a studio in Fulham Broadway, London. I played keyboards, sang and created beats by then, but I wasn't experienced in using a sound deck. Alex, the kind German engineer showed me the way.

Over the next two-and-a-half-years, I commuted from Windsor to Fulham Broadway to complete this record. I even asked two friends from Brigidine Covent School to sing backup. By 1995, the album was done and even completed my first solo gig. I chose an Etonian band as my support knowing they pulled girls too.

Crystal sent me a wedding invitation (so it was her my prediction was for) when Johnny came to town. He was telling me about his new band, Republica, and I told him I was heading back to LA. At the wedding reception, at the Super Bowl stadium, I met with Crystal's father again. He was so happy and amazed I came. I hid around a huge plant while the couple had their wedding photos taken on the Super Bowl pitch. Finally Sandy walked in and jumped out to surprise Crystal. She was so happy. The wedding reception was incredible and my first LA love who I met at the beach in 87, now married. Mrs Crystal Lee Barnel was older, happier. I don't remember how long I was in LA that time but I did visit Big Bear on this visit which was an incredible experience.

Chapter 8 — Beached Up

It was all happening in London in 95 when 'Cool Britannia' era exploded. Indie music and bands Oasis, Blur, Pulp and pop groups like The Spice Girls hit huge sales. I had now run dry in Old Windsor and Sandra couldn't watch me chasing rainbows much longer. Johnny is now my mate and offered me to move into his Ladbroke Grove apartment in Notting Hill. His home seemed to be a hub where many of the indie stars passed through. The number of well-known faces I met, saw and sat chatting with got ridiculous.

Arriving at Holland Park tube in 1995 was my mark of leaving everything in the past I hope, at least for now. Notting Hill was where stars hideout. On the very first day from the tube to meet Johnny, I felt nervous and landed with a thud from LA. It felt from one hazy day into a storm of guitars, drugs and expensive lunches.

The next three years followed with, what I could only call, hedonism in the rock degree. I lived centre in the middle of an era that passed the mirror right for the next pop tart to roll their £20. Cocaine was like finding winter in the middle of your soul for any season. Freedom felt heightened with your tongue on double time. I had never seen so much white powder but if ten were here for dinner, I mean winter, it was just enough. I was never into drugs and never thought about it but, it was everywhere in the scene at this time.

I was the psychic butler of Notting Hill, so it felt, but a musician too. I loved Johnny. We were close though he was facing his own inner fights with desire, music and touring. During this time, I was in a routing of returning to LA then back to Notting Hill. I had the time of my life by the end of the 1990s but living practically homeless and penniless, travel goes by like a flash. The lyrics, "You're born then you live and you die. You get one try & I've tried everything," from Republica's track, *Try Everything*, rang so true to this time.

I had my last stint in Windsor in 1998. I arrived at Heathrow from LA and dropped my bags, and ran to a psychic fair for quick cash. I was the only one sitting at a table with no tools like Tarot or crystals. Two girls took my eye and a stunning petite, dark haired Malaysian girl struck me. Her name was Michelle Artiss, and I recall how my Nan told me my next girlfriend was an artist with the name of Artiss. This came to me when I connected to the spirit world muttering in bed six months before.

"Nan, who will my next girlfriend be?"

"The words, Jolyon you will meet a girl. She's an artist. Michelle, half Malaysian and British. So pretty, born in Lambeth. She is living with her mum and stepdad in Denham, Buckinghamshire in England." We had an instant connection. She was sensitive who seemed to get me. Three weeks later though, I was due to head out to LA again as I was booked up with readings for a further three weeks.

In the fast lane of my life, commuting seemingly monthly, Johnny's just had a major hit with *Ready to Go*. He explained that a passing comment to girlfriend Anne Shenton inspired the title. "Are you ready to go? It's my memory and I'm wide awake in winter." LA is home to my heart and I tried to make my music dreams a reality there by sending copies of my first solo album to the best. I blagged my way into some record label offices. I had

Johnny to assist me on a few Head of A&R department names to approach.

I stayed at Jim's 'At The Beach' hostel this time. It was cheap and a stride to the ocean and this inspired me to take countless phone calls and handwrite letters to labels and execs for the next week. On this trip, real life happened both good and bad. I was not a tourist anymore but commuting, trying to get heard and one day, live and recount the back street, faded, dry grass gardens of Venice. Magical walks, maxed credit cards and new friends, and buying dead men's ID green cards for $40 were real.

Arjen Hartman was a wild Guns and Roses blonde, Dutch guy who I met one morning at the communal breakfast area at Jim's.

"What do you do?" he asked.

"I'm a psychic and musician," I replied.

"A magician?"

"No, a musician."

"What, you can speak to the dead?"

"Well I can hear and receive messages from them, yes."

"I don't believe all that," Arjen added but used harsher words. I raged after he tried to belittle me. I was not taking it. I said his grandmother was to my left, annoyed and I mentioned her name. A week later, he swam too far in the sea and the strong dip current pulled him further out. With all his tough strength and wild man floors, no one helped him out. He recounts giving up and explained feeling bolted out of the sea to arrive on the sand. Was this this his spiritual learning, or his grandmother giving him a hint of how real it all is? We became close friends after this and travelled home together not before maxing out one another's credit card to get tickets home.

Yearly, thousands try to discover their soul in the burnt grass of LA GRIDS. After weeks of LA mishaps, readings and cheap liquor Arjen and I head to Santa Monica mall to buy coats in the 90 degree weather as it was raining in Europe. We hoped for the best. We boarded and sat on our bucket seats aboard a CityBird flight to Brussels where we would part for the time being. Sitting in this plane, Arjen seemed unresolved in his own search for stardom and girls. Also a musician, he mastered in facility management, whatever that was. He tried to apply for at least fifty jobs or more weekly from the local library which we walked in the blazing heat and to no avail.

During his downtime, Arjen preferred to play soccer with his other mates from Japan or go wild as we did often in Sunset Boulevard. I remember one of our friends brought a beaten car for $300 painted in hippy bright design. I bet it was left behind by the last hopeful with rock designs. Six of us in total all stacked into this car in total dress up of sorts as we hit some clubs. Often as these nights went, Arjen would go missing with some Jack and Coke and end up, as you do, with a pretty model giving him her business card. He usually could not recall what happened and thought she was a whore — well, I bettered his approach to a high class escort. It finally transpired she was a successful commercial print model.

I had done my job on this trip and performed many psychic readings at $150 for forty-five minutes a time while Arjen and the rest of his clan had to do with trekking for an hour to possibly an unwise side of central LA, to shovel gravel. For more than eight hours a day at $80, they returned to the hostel looking broken, covered in grey dirt, annoyed to know I'd make another $150 in the morning.

87

We were though, all living on the best side of our lives in a town we called Hope which would throw you no lifeline but a dead man's old ID on North of Broadway (Downtown) in daylight at $40. Defeating this, you may need to take a trip past borderlines even faster and scarier after the refreshed momentary breeze of San Diego, before Mexico City. You were half mad if you chanced this, but Arjen was wild and his best friend, not so, hoped the fuck if anyone of them died trying to have a clear credit card.

The flight back was bumpy and I wore an army style fitted jacket I brought along with a coat that day in the mall and Arjen in a new leather rock jacket. We ordered so many Jack Daniels on the flight until Arjen took the window seat and passed out, leaving him to his dreams. Parting at Brussels was weird. We had been on some wild adventures that looking back seemed hard.

But we would see each other again in LA. I had been signed years before as a model and auditioned for a 7UP commercial there. I met some great new friends in LA and other dreamers from all over the world, and on another further trip after returning with Arjen, I was back three weeks later. Jim, the owner of the hostel, took a chosen eight people on board his boat down from Marina Del across to Malibu.

My passport and American immigration law allowed me to reside in the country three months at a time and I did more work then returned, which became a routine. I spent what seemed months in LA between 97 and 98, my new address was a few blocks south of Melrose where I met Olivia almost a decade before.

Back in the UK, Johnny returned from tour exhausted and Anne was nowhere to be seen. Johnny asked if I wanted to hit the town for the afternoon. He knew that three weeks ago, I was in LA happy with a job offer to work for a psychic telephone service called Twin Vision America. After another expensive rock star lunch we reached a travel agent and he wondered if I still wanted to do that job in LA.

"What? Yes, why?"

"I'll buy you a ticket."

The next week I was in LA, wearing a phone headset giving psychic readings to clients calling from all over the United States. On this occasion, I was in LA for about three months. It was December and a cool 30 Degrees. Michelle planned to come over the following week. The following day however, my phone rang I answered to the sound of Johnny saying, "Hiya, Where are you?"

"What? I'm in LA."

"Yeah, but where?"

"Umm, Sunset across the street called Orange and Fountain."

"Hey Saff," Johnny asked Saffron, lead singer of Republica off the phone. "Where is Orange and Fountain?"

"About four blocks away," she replied.

"What. What, oh my God, where are you Jon?"

I hear the sounds of him laughing, "We're here, come over," he added. Johnny's here and I wondered if he planned this all along. What happened next was amazing. I recall on the phone he asked, "What are you doing for New Year's Eve?" I replied "Nothing special." He then asked if Michelle and I would like to join him to Marilyn Manson's Party in the desert, which I jumped at the chance.

I met many popstars in the last year or so but even before, I met some before they became famous. One encounter, in 1995, staying across the road from me in Old Windsor was

Sarah Cracknell's mum's home. Sarah, from the band Saint Etienne was also the daughter of Stanley Kubrick's first assistant director Derek Cracknell.

A 15 year old Donna Air, then one half of pop duo Crush with Aussie Jayni Hoy also lived nearby. Johnny and his Merry Men penned pop tracks *Loved Up* and *Jellyhead*, yet I was unsure if they understood the content. Donna and Jayni were open to seeing what they had instore for them, yet both were set beyond pop. Donna used to come over to Johnny's with her predicted boyfriend and I visited them in Blackheath once. I bumped into her in Kings Road fifteen years later and passed pleasantries.

Windsor was home to some names all who were now making big strides far away from there — as far as Europe and the USA. Sarah I'd known for some time and she invited me over to her old flat in Old Windsor with her then boyfriend Mick Bund of the band Mexico 70. I was the baby of this troop, the last one aiming my synths out of Windsor.

But did make my strides away to LA again with Johnny Male, Tim Dorney and Saffron Sprackling. It was December 30th, 1998 and Michelle had just arrived. Life felt better. Michelle and I grabbed a cab to meet our British mates, arriving at the Sky hotel off Sunset Boulevard opposite the Rainbow Club. I was so happy to see Johnny and he escorted Michelle and me to the pool up on the roof where Tim was having a whale of a time. Saff joined us and we eventually called for a cab and went off to Burbank for dinner. Burbank was an amazing area, mainly consisting of huge white buildings full of studios. Republica were working with producer Ben Grosse and mixing their second album *Speed Ballads*. It was lovely to have dinner with all my mates in LA.

The next day was New Year's Eve, and by 7pm, Michelle and I made our way back to Republica's hotel all dressed up. Michelle wore her eight inch heels from Trashy Lingerie Hollywood and a gorgeous red Chinese dress. Johnny opened a bottle of champagne to start the celebrations in his room while we wait for Tim and Saff. Johnny was on great form and excitedly sung his merits and played the new Devine Comedy album.

We joined Tim downstairs, and later Saff was joined with her then boyfriend Fast from American band, Fun Lovin' Criminals. Michelle and I shared Saff's car with Fast at the wheel. We followed behind with Tim, Johnny and Ben who made sparks climbing the Hollywood foothills in the low Ferrari. I remember we drove for a good half hour, stopping, turning around, trying another route until a call came through to Saff's mobile saying that Drew (Barrymore) had gone to Leonardo's (DiCaprio) party and that we were now heading to Gwen Stafani's place. When we finally arrived the road that was extremely sloped and there were rows and rows of cars. Finally we hiked the last 500 yards, Michelle battled in heels as I reached my hand to help.

Gwen's house from the outside was built like most of the homes on this part of the hill — bespoke, like a mini castle and the path to the door was lit by hundreds of white Christmas lights. As we walked in, straight away I noticed a few celebrities. I had a glimpse of Amanda De Cadenet, and model Tyra Banks. The house was vast, yet cosy with a stunning hallway that had a lit fire and sofas. Once we got used to where we was, I found myself, Saff, Fast and

Michelle raising our own glasses early, alone as the time difference to the UK meant we were behind and we toasted at the same time London would.

Gwen, with her curly platinum bob make sure were all having fun and told us to help ourselves to drinks, and drifts off to attend to her other guests. I had been introduced as Republica's drummer for the evening on the door entry and Michelle being my plus one. Fast was lovely and we chat as Michelle and Saff mingled. Then I was directed to the bathroom, as apparently it would have been my ideal one. When I entered this huge bathroom, it had tropical plants and a curved entry to the gold coloured toilet. It was more like a gorgeous star's dressing room than the powder room. The night passed and the rest would be a bit of a blur, but what an amazing evening.

On the following day we all decided to go to Santa Monica and hit the parade of stores while Johnny and Tim hit the English pub on First Street. We wandered and bought a t-shirt or two while I showed Saff some hidden gems. The next day, I joined Tim and Johnny for drinks in Sunset Boulevard at the Irish bar and had some very interesting mixes. Tim and Johnny were a double act of wit and humour and I was exhausted to keep up. We decided to head back much later to find Saff and hit the hotel's hidden bar (The Sky Bar) owned by Johnny Depp — not to be confused by The Viper Room. It was tiny and here, we had a round of Bloody Mary's. They were strong, I mean strong. It still remains an amazing time to reflect back on. This was about my tenth visit to LA and two more would follow, but in 1998, I had my mates with me and for that time it was, in Tim's words, "remarkable".

My friends were all back home in London though not before an amazing day at music producer Ben Grosse's studio in Burbank. It was close to where I auditioned for a part in a boyband years before. Ben was a big producer at the time and I asked him if he'd give my latest track *Nebula Blue*, recorded in a dusty basement studio in Clapham, London, weeks before.

I managed to perform Nebula Blue on the infamous Gong Show close to Fountain and Orange near Westwood Village in Hollywood. I was paid $500 to be heckled the loudest in front of a live audience. They shrieked as I came on blazed in neo dark, long, military coat and blue hair wax with matching blue make-up.

I sung "something you're predicting will leave critics alone". A carefully positioned bikini clad model sat side left in-front of me, an attempt to put me off. Though I winked and made a look knowing it would lead the cameramen to follow my eye. I added a move which was to look up left to indicate a problem I noticed with lighting. I kept this movement and almost waited on cue, in beat with a chord change. This looked good from the audiences view and added a mystery to my performance. My friends were back home working for BT or other low key jobs, but I was on Rodeo Drive with smudged blue make-up.

The remanence of my performance that night, chasing my dream like a crazy. I stitched the lifestyle I wanted and insisted I must invent and build up survival tactics, though I was scared, excited and intensely lonely. I had almost been mugged at knife point in 1995 at North on Broadway across from City Hall, Downtown. Being poor, once at Christmas 1998, I eat eight cent ramen noodles for five weeks, which now seemed madness considering I partied with Gwen Stefani shortly afterwards. That caused me to have a disease which meant sometimes, I couldn't swallow and my throat would spasm and appeared to choke.

Despite this, a resolute Saff came to visit me and I gave her a reading, then walked up to Hollywood Boulevard and stopped at a diner and chatted. She said I looked ill and thin and confided in her that I worked so hard to make things happen. I was almost penniless but it'd be worse when I return to London. Saff said she was sure Johnny would allow me to stay in his Notting Hill house when we got back. My next saviour to come, once I got home, would be myself, and a popstar of yesteryear. One thing in life at this time was, I had connections in rocky places. That's what chasing your dreams was about, kids!

By 1999, I left Johnny's place again though I'd be back there later. I moved to share a house with flamboyant painter Freddy Thuon. His home, just off All Saints Road, was streets away from Johnny's place. 90s female pop outfit All Saints adopted their name from here not long before. Stephen (Tin Tin) Duffy, the original singer for Duran Duran, lived on All Saints above a shop with his girlfriend at this time.

Freddy was an eccentric type of cross dressing, soft natured person, who could switch personalities and become, for me, a living nightmare. He stayed up until 3am most days whilst I worked late giving phone readings. Johnny was on the last leg of a long tour and I was looking more at my own life. Johnny became a brother in some ways, yet I needed to get off the ride. I lived in the middle of the scene, but it was over.

A year before, I met Richard Norris, another musician and friend of Johnny's. Richard had been in 90s dance group The Grid. I first came across his music in Our Price Window record store in Maidenhead years before. Richard was a lovely guy, serene intelligent and witty. One evening in 98, myself, Johnny, Richard and a couple of others all went together to a local pub in Kensal Rise. Richard mentioned he was not aware I was a musician as well as a psychic. Richard seemed interested and invited me over to his then home in a street jokingly named 'Stella Street', in reference to a TV comedy where stars lived on one street. Chris Martin from Coldplay lived here with his then future wife Gwyneth Paltrow, among others.

Visiting Richard's was always a fun experience. He had a room full of vinyl synthesisers, robots, and a recording console. I brought along one of my latest tracks — an instrumental version of Dark Lolita. After a couple of listens, he stood there and said he wanted to help produce the final version. He then left the room while I stood with a smile and then he returned with another friend. Richard felt if he were to produce it, he could only improve it by five percent, but loved what I had to offer.

Chapter 9 — Near Nirvana

Later in 1999, following a private reading for Richard, he invited me over for a party at his. His friends and other people in music and fashion were there. No-one could have ever known what was about to transpire. As the evening progressed I was starting to feel a presence in the room and almost got up and asked everyone to go quiet. Explaining I felt a gentleman's spirit here, the following was later documented in detail by Richard, who took a transcript of the whole event to his contact in New York who knew facts about Kurt Cobain.

This presence grew in my mind and I began just speaking and saying, "I have a guy here he is not blonde anymore, it is light brown. He said he attempted coming through to me twice before and this was his third. This man spoke about his love for his child and his passions, including mainly music."

As the details drifted out from me, he gave his name as Kurt Cobain. This seemed a shock to all though the guys seemed captivated. I reeled out detail after detail and went around the room with private messages for all. It was a lovely and strange end to an evening but we all raised our glasses to Kurt and drifted off home.

Richard Norris was not performing at this time rather reviewing recent vinyl releases. He started to work for a new Soho based Internet Company. They were thinking of setting up a psychic engine to add to the company site. He called me up and explained and we agreed to meet at a bar near his office where all deals, including record deal, were notoriously agreed over a drink or two. He explained what it was all about and what it involved.

The following week, I was introduced to the whole team and was allocated a little desk. Here, I would collate as much information about the psychic industry I learnt. Surfing the internet and looking in magazine of rhythm of psychic adverts. I drew up long documents and figures with stats and ideas. I was on a retainer and this felt great to have a set amount of money paid for six months, something I never had. This gave me the freedom to start to look for my own flat in London, after years of jumping from sofa to sofa. I saw a tiny postcard in a newsagent in Notting Hill and made an appointment to view a studio flat in near Holland Park. It was good enough and I had keys to come and go for the first time in my life. Michelle moved in with me and things were nice.

Michelle travelled an hour from our home and often returned late in the evening. The company Richard worked for had a PR agency deal with an old contact whose offices were on Wardour Street in Soho, above a sex shop. Richard explained to their Director, David that he thought I could become a big name and wanted to start filming a documentary. We watched a video of a new artist he was about to promote. At the time, he looked after British singers, artists and now actresses like Martine McCutcheon from *EastEnders* and later the film *Love Actually*, and teen pop upstart Billie Piper, famed later for her starring role in TV success *The Secret Diaries of a Call Girl*. I was their first only psychic-musician and set about a plan to get me out there and be known.

Quickly after that meeting, David called me saying he set up a meeting with Rav, The Gossip columnist at *News of the World*. The evening before I did some automatic writing about Rav. I sealed and signed on and inserted in an envelope my predictions for him inside. In the cab on route to meet Rav, I gave David the envelope and I sat back, trying to relax. David explained if I could impress him, I could do anything.

Whilst I waited outside the office, David had a word before I was due to meet Rav. Shortly, David appeared out and said, "We have go, I'll explain in the car." He added whatever I wrote in my reading struck and shocked Rav on the spot. It, as David put, "Almost overrode him and wasn't ready to meet, or for the reality of what I was able to do."

David called me quite quickly after that event saying he had great news about an interview for a woman's magazine. Before the day of the interview, David called and read a list of celebrity names including Madonna for me to do automatic writings for. I was nervous as it was a new area yet Michelle offered me assurances. Michelle was such a support always, though music, chasing my dreams and even following me on stage to play keyboards from 2000 to 2007. In her car one morning, I call David and relayed my predictions and hope. To his surprise, weeks later, a three page feature transpired in Marie Claire. It was unheard of, he explained, and very happy about my talents.

Christmas approached and I was in touch with Arjen from Holland and he invited us to join him and his friends in Hengelo for New Years. It had been a year since I last saw him and thought it would be a good catch up. We were like LA brothers. Michelle arranged for us first to visit and stay at her aunt's place at Hague. The morning we left to catch a train to meet Arjen, I dressed in a blue plastic, long jacket and taped neon glow.

I'll never forget my expression when, as the train seemed to travel forever across flat, black earth lands, I arrived. It seemed in Hengelo everyone was into GNR or Nirvana as reflected in their style. We did our best to fit in though I soon noticed how Arjen, in some ways, was seen as an outsider in his home town. I think he had seen more of the world than they did, which may have affected the way they viewed him. I knew he would leave soon for new adventures. My memories were mixed about Hengelo, but I recalled thinking we went all that way to sit in a room watching fireworks on TV. How on earth would I explain later if I ever were to have kids? "Where did you spent New Year's in 1999, dad?" "Watching TV in Hengelo!"

In February of 2001, I was offered my own column for *It's Fate* magazine. Here, I wrote celebrity predictions five month before publications where I predicted examples like David Beckham would break his left ankle in the World Cup the following year. My editor Mary Bryce was brilliant, a wonderful lady who adored Keith Richards. Money was becoming difficult in this year as Michelle and I were balancing living costs with infrequent work patterns. Michelle was an incredible artist and, along with her work partner, both ran an events company.

Our tenancy was up for renewal and we were having difficulties in this place including living next to very noisy neighbours. Michelle and I were struggling so she decided to leave and I stayed on one final month. A few weeks before this, Saff called to ask if I would do a reading for one of her friends, not realising it was Siobhan Fahey. She had been one third of 80s super group Bananarama. Arriving at her house, I explained that I connect with spirit, and if she was not comfortable with this she could stop me at any time. We stayed in touch and even met up socially on occasion.

My time in Holland Park was becoming so hard to manage, I was desperate to leave and low on cash. I called Siobhan in tears from a phone box on Kensington High Street and explained. She offered me to live with her. She had decorators at her home almost every day renovating the basement flat for which I moved in for a few months.

Music was still very strong in my mind, even through my turmoil. I made sure I kept recording. At the back of the garden was a small out house that was turned into a recording studio, kitted out with the latest computer software. This including a vintage Roland drum machine, used for GNR's album *DANCE* that had got me through my school days.

Chapter 10 — Tears In Rain

My reputation as a psychic seemed to spread among the Primrose set I frequently read for a celebrity or two. Soon an old connection was about to be reconnected. I had, by this time, made new friends including Pearl Lowe ('Sam' to her friend), singer for 90s band Powder. She's now married to the drummer from super indie rockers Supergrass. We got on instantly, yet I couldn't help but find myself holding professional secrets of many. Jude Law lived just behind Siobhan's road with wife Sadie Frost. I remember being woken up once to join a party downstairs where the gathering was made up with chart toppers and actresses.

Pearl and I slowly became friends and I would visit her many times and even once met a young Daisy Lowe. One more name was to be added to this NW3 line up, grunge rocker, Gavin Rossdale, frontman of band Bush, who was dating Gwen Stefani and someone Pearl introduced me to. Gavin later revealed by press to be the father of Daisy. Pearl mentioned he would like a reading and told him how I worked and that I was also a musician and trusted.

I made my way to Gavin's house a week later in Primrose Hill. I waited outside his home until he pulled up in a blacked out Range Rover asking if I had a pen.

"No, I'm not a fan. I'm Jolyon, the psychic here to read you."

"Oh, great quick come in. There's paps everywhere."

His home was a second floor flat and had this wonderful huge centre table on which I was to read him. He had a huge, black dog called Winston, and a room full of guitars and recording gear. Gavin had a lovely, warm nature and spoke about music until I began the reading. He seemed very surprised and happy, and asked if he could see me in future. We agreed and returned at a future date. I hadn't mention that I spent New Year's at Gwen's home in Hollywood in 1998 of which he may have been there.

While I cannot mention his predictions here, I did mention he would marry Gwen and twice! It was New York City and London locations I was seeing for their nuptials so they could please both sets of parents living on both sides of the world. I think I became known as the rock star psychic, and friend which felt nice.

Back at Siobhan's, on Sundays, her son's mates came over — usually Bono (of U2)'s kids. Soon I moved on from Siobhan's home at the same time builders were finished. I did, by the end of my stay, managed to complete recording an album in the garden studio entitled *SENSYON:Approaching*, adopting Sensyon as my then stage name. I went then to live with a lady in Englands Road around the corner. She was an energetic, fun property agent who had an even more energetic son but it was later recognised he suffered from ADHD. I stayed here for about eight weeks. I was working on a phone line for an American psychic phone line company at this time, based in Topanga Canyon, LA. Once the receptionist there suggested I should come out and work from office and stay in Los Angeles again. Around this time I was thinking it was time to return to my heartland. I ran out of options and sofas, so I booked myself a ticket a week later.

Arriving back in LA, I was excited and slightly nervous yet boarded the bus to arrive at the offices in the afternoon. I think I picked up a bug and felt very ill fast and made my way first to the pharmacy and later being met by a gentlemen from the office. I don't think they actually expected me though they knew my arrival time as my boss wouldn't be there until the following day. I worked from the office taking calls from all over the US. A lady explained we don't have anywhere for you to stay so I booked myself into a cheap motel down the road. This was a real dive with a dry pool that looked like it had many unsolved murders and prostitutes stay.

A nicer girl from the office seemed worried and offered to help me find a better place to stay. That evening, while on the freeway in her car, I started to feel a great pain coming from my chest and I clenched my hands. I was fading fast. Five minutes later she took me to the hospital and started to speed to 80 miles per hour in a 50mph speed limit. A police outrider caught up as she gestures to him "heart attack, heart attack." We were given siren escort to the nearest hospital and rushed into emergency, with heart monitors attached to my chest.

Once my heart was calmed, I was asked to sign a form agreeing the price of $50,000 for medical bills. All my LA visits and I didn't have medical insurance, crazy. I don't know how but I ripped the wires off my chest and ran. My female friend said I was crazy but I had CODES. Her boyfriend turned up in his pimped car and wanted to know why his girlfriend was driving this English kid around at 1am.

That night, I slept on the floor of the office, and in the morning the boss's wife said I shouldn't have slept the way I did. Furthermore the boss finally met me and called me into his office. Of course we hadn't met so you could imagine how bad this first impression felt for me. I drifted in half dead and pale from my murmur and night on the floor. He produced a copy of a commercial they were going to use to advertise their company. I didn't seem impressed as he felt the same as I explained about my illness, and that they treated me so badly by not respecting this. He got up and asked me to get out of his office and building.

On the way out, I said to all the staff, "You are crazy to work for such a human being. He doesn't give a shit about you, just money."

I stormed out and walked back to my motel in the sheer heat, grabbed my things and caught a cab to The Cadillac Hotel on Venice Beach. I knew the area; loved the beach and wanted to get the hell out of the motel. I felt slightly more comfortable knowing I was back in control although I was, by this time, so very ill, shaking. I checked in and rang Michelle who seemed very scared and concerned. She was so good at sorting things and called me back to explain that, providing I'd get a letter to prove I received medical attention, I could fly back to the UK according to 'rule 68'. This allowed me to use my fixed return ticket back to grey Heathrow Airport sooner rather than later.

Dear Johnny Male seemed shocked when speaking to me on the phone. He was in a restaurant with the other members of Republica when hearing about my ordeal. As I tried to speak with a shaky voice, but all I heard was him saying out of the phone, "Shh, it's the butler, he's had a heart attack," while also offering any support I needed.

The next morning I was determined not to waste the fact I was in LA and got a bus out, intentionally, to Beverly Hills, but instead I got off at Sunset Boulevard. I went into the infamous Guitar Centre and Hustler store then rested. Outside, I sat on the low wall at strip club The Body Shop, which was closed on that day. Suddenly, I heard loudly to my left, "Jolyon." I could not believe it was one of Johnny's ex-girlfriend from London, a photographer.

She said, "Oh my God, what are you doing here? You look terrible, what's happened?" She insisted I'd go with her to The Standard Hotel where she and her work crew were staying. They were, that night, off to shoot for a Diesel campaign in the desert. Walking through the hotel foyer, I saw models next to the windows while I was all in black in the hot sun. Still shaking she brought me a cocktail and offered me her room after my crazy trip.

"Stay Jolyon as we're leaving later, I'll call Jon," Johnny's ex added. The next morning, at my own hotel Michelle called to say it's been sorted for my arrival back to London the next day. In the morning I got myself together very slowly away from a place full of great memories, but couldn't muster the energy to even smile. I met a guy I recognised from a UK television show who noticed me looking so ill. He was so kind and wanted to stay with me until my taxi came to take me to LAX airport.

At the airport, I was aware that I didn't have all the papers required to fly — only a prescription note and medication. I walked up to this lovely older ground staff officer about to celebrate his retirement with his enthusiastic colleagues. I explained my situation to him and he said "Don't worry." He then, after looking at me, added, "Looks like we need to get you home." I was told I'd be sitting at the back of the plane with the stewardesses so they could keep an eye on me. I ended up reading them all which even took our minds off my illness.

We landed into Heathrow and before I exited the plane, one of the crew members gave me a huge bottle of champagne. Michelle met me and explained that she had to take me straight to hospital to adhere to medical travel law. The hospital would then send a letter to the US so I would not end up with a huge legal bill, saving me a huge sum. The nurse, who Michelle and I dubbed 'the sexy one', stuck this huge needle into my bum, gave me drugs and medications, and monitored me. I loved Michelle and felt safe around her as she drove me to stay with her sister Caroline outside Denham, Berkshire where I rested in the odd, freezing and dark surrounding.

I stayed here for a few weeks and this period gave me the freedom to start looking at my options once more. I started by purchasing myself a 1984 silver BMW for £50 from my old friend Richard Cox in Ascot. One morning, while checking my emails, I saw an email from my editor Mary Bryce, with the subject heading 'Big Brother' which I had almost deleted. She asked if I was interested in auditioning as the Resident Psychic on UK reality panel show *Big Brother's Little Brother* for Channel 4. Apparently, they saw up to 96 psychics without finding an ideal person so I thought I'd give it a go.

Chapter 11 — Broken Mic

On my audition day with Big Brother, I was picked up outside my then home in Hampstead, London and be driven to Elstree Studios in Borehamwood. I'm dressed in a black suit and its boiling but I had to keep the image going.

Upon arrival, I was greeted in a room full of crew and sound technicians. They explained the process of the day, how the show would progress and my involvement in it. I also wanted to practice on the room. I began by just staring at the interviewer and connected with spirit. His face seemed startled. I then, without plan, went down the table and read everyone all in the room. There was this one woman I took out in particular and gave her information with such detail, she almost dropped her boom and ran out of the room. The job was in the bag.

On my first day on the show, I was ushered to a dressing room until called on set. I sat with Dermot O'Leary who was very friendly, said hello and shook my hand, as we waited for his producer's cues as the show began. During the filming, I was asked to guess who I'd think would win that year. With no information about these contestants at all, I said "A female, tanned with dark hair."

After the show, the driver dropped me outside an off-license to get a drink. When I looking for something inside, the shop manager behind the till if that was my car outside. As I was about to answer, I noticed a bunch of girls banging on the door. I had fans — oh my God, already — how? The driver gradually got me back into the Mercedes and drove me around the corner home.

After my stint on Big Brother, music was my mind and I decided, along with Michelle on keyboards, to gig, performing tracks from the Sensyon album. This gig, near Putney at The Kings Head music venue, was a bit of a dive like many on the London circuit. The idea of these was to grab the attention of music A&R scouts.

I went on stage with all the effects and Michelle lit, looking great eye candy on synths. Half way through the set my guitar was cutting in and out. Though only two songs to go in my set and I threw my guitar into the air for a friend to catch. My radio mic also failed and in my head, I couldn't wait for it to end. But the mic came back on and we were into my next song, *Domination*. The original version was recorded years before in Kilburn. It's a catchy number about a psychic having the power to control dictators and bring them to their knees — wouldn't that be a great day! This track was written while Saddam Hussein was still in power.

I walked off stage feeling exhausted and a bit down. Though as I reappeared from the backstage, I noticed a welcome old ghost from the last year or so — Richard Norris.

"Hello, buddy. Wow, you came, thank you. Sorry about the technical," I said.

"Ah, it adds to a set sometimes," he laughed.

Richard then explained he bought a copy of my performance from the sound guy who had been recording bands in case they wanted one.

A week passed and Richard called me at home asking me more about my song, *Domination*. He explained he started an independent record label with Andy Chatterley, a producer I met a year before through Richard, and later went on to score hits for The Pussycat Dolls and more. Richard added they are making an electro compilation album and wanted me to re-record *Domination*.

Only two weeks later I met with Andy with an update about the record. The studio was within an old trading company building estate in London. I felt almost aware this place was haunted and had a tense feeling due to whatever other business that had been going on in other units here. The recording session was fun, stressful and strange. Here I was in a vocal booth about to sing a brand new version of my own song. It took about an hour or so and when I included the piano section in the middle 8, and later signed a publishing agreement, that was the end of that session. I go home with the agreement in my bag, feeling happy as I rode passed the business district of Canary Wharf in east London. On the Overground rail, I thought that finally, it's all about music.

Life went back to normal for a while until Michelle and I were told that the all of Richard's label acts were to be shot for a magazine called Sleaze Nation in Regents Park. Old friend Siobhan Fahey, also signed onto the label, would be in the shoot too. It was baking hot on the day of the shoot and I wore my black, padded, synthetic wrap round futuristic jacket and black Marilyn Manson style boots. It looked a bit odd while others were in bikinis enjoying ice cream. Michelle wore a cheerleader ensemble. Other bands were in all oddities that London can offer. After the shoot, we attracted quite a crowd as we sit with them and enjoyed an ice pop, then we said all our goodbyes.

Michelle and I were closer than ever before but like any other solid relationship, we had our problems. Weeks before the shoot, we planned to take the August Bank Holiday away at her dad's mobile beach home in Durdle Door, Dorset which looked out to the sea. We arrived around 9pm, settled down, slept and woke to enjoy the sun and sand, and we set up a BBQ. But we would argue about the smallest things. We spoke about splitting a few times, but I didn't really want this. I wanted her, I loved her but she seemed lost. We had been there for one another from the day we met at the psychic fair years before. Michelle made things seem possible, safe and when I ever felt scared she offered me that important assurance.

While we drove back to London, Michael Jackson's song *Don't Walk Away* came on as we flew over Chiswick Bridge. I felt emotional and just hoped we'd be ok. How would I be without Michelle? Where would she be if I needed to see her? I couldn't think about all this. We were just tired, confused and Michelle's had been driving all day, hot and bothered. That night we went to bed and I held her tight and said "I love you." Time passed unscathed and together we collected our copy of Sleaze Nation and found the label story titled 'God Made Me Hardcore'. The story was good apart from the fact they had only gone and misspelt my name. That got us some press attention when Michelle and I were photographed at some clubs and appeared in different publications. Slowly I felt we were living separate lives, even though I still loved her and we performed together.

Chapter 12 — Invisible Sun

Since I was 12, after all the mountains I climbed, I knew myself and my strengths. Though I never realised that after the bullying and emotional challenges during my teenage and early adult years that there was about to be another great challenge ahead. I lived this life the best way I could, going from obstacle and taping situations together to get through. The next few years were about using all I had learnt to try and stitch a new life together.

Michelle and I were still very close though after I was hired as a glamour photographer helping models to form a portfolio, I started to scout for new talents. My first client was a young nineteen year old model, pictures of her were taken at a close friend's gorgeous home in the Chelsea area and the photos turned out really nice. My next model was someone I met six months before whilst scouting for dancers for which I needed for an upcoming gig to back me on stage. Nikka was a tall, peroxide blonde from the Czech Republic. She was warm, kind and unlike how models are stereotypically perceived. She came over to the Notting Hill house I lived in previously, and took some glamour pics. As I walked her back to the tube and said "Thanks, I'll be in touch," a storm was about to end my relationship with Michelle.

I returned to the house to discover Michelle on the phone in tears and pain discussing the shoot as she was not happy with the content and was worried there was more to this. She announced that we could not carry on and I sat, slumped in shock and fear and asked me to move out. Nikka and I were only ever friends, nothing more. Though this was too much for my Michelle. The following day we went to Oxford Street and as we were walking out of HMV record store the song *Fix You* by Coldplay was being streamed loudly. This just raised my emotions and I held back my tears. On the bus coming home we were silent yet holding hands whilst I was crying behind my dark sun glasses in pain. She could tell and we were both obviously in pain yet still loved each other. Two weeks later I heard that I had been offered a new home and made plans to view.

By this time, Michelle and I were still very much very good friends. Though, I possessed a secret, not so deep, which had been eating at me since I was 12, was just about to surface from those tearful exhausting teenage years. And this was something I couldn't open up to Michelle about.

I was not gay or ever thought about it. I looked after and cared for guys in anyway and I found I was talking to them motherly. My look was sometimes alternative. In my teens, I always studied the looks, face structure, and hair of girls. I was always pushing the barriers through the years, and my look and image altered from rock guy to androgynous alien to feminine guy. It was in August 2005 while assisting at the auditions for the new Michael Jackson musical Thriller, written and produced by my friend Adrian Grant, I recall thinking I didn't know what to wear, as a guy, anymore. I wore a black suit or girls 'velour tracksuit pants' and guy jacket or UGG Boots. Really, I was over being a man and admitted what I wanted since I was about 12 — to be a girl.

I made this call during relationship turmoil as Michelle and I had officially broken up. We tried one too many times to fix each other but we couldn't. That said, she was open minded about my image change and would be with me during this process over the following years.

It was such an odd time, and a few months after I fulfilled, what some arguably said was a strange decision, a duty to audition and perform in adult movies. I don't really remember for how long but it was such an organised world — very opposite to the public's perception. I turned up to the filming of my first film a little excited and slightly nervous, but noticed how professional the set was and performers would spend hours upon hours sitting around waiting finally for their scene.

I became reputable in the field and having done a few movies, I was told by a producer that I were to be a professional and receive higher fees. On a set in West Kensington, a nice laidback guy mentioned he had always wanted to produce his own movie and asked if I would help. We met up a week later and I realised how seriously he was taking this so I took this opportunity further with him. We met up for meetings with figures, wrote a Performer Wish list, and set out location budgets. It got to the point I was so engaged into this, I drew up professional performer contracts and called agencies to book girls. There were long fifteen hour days over two months of shooting. I recalled at the end of a shoot, at the Riverside Hotel opposite the Houses of Parliament, we wrapped up shoot at midnight. My business partner Terry and I made our way to the bar. We could hardly speak as we were so tired but we felt the sense of great accomplishment.

Yet, during this point, my inner, intense feelings about my gender heightened so much, I made an appointment with my GP. I walked into her office and at first I just sat in silence as I could not quite say what I wanted. Once I gathered my thoughts I announced that I wanted to be a girl. I had known most of my life and it added up but, it was getting loud and clear. We spoke in depth and I was referred to see a male specialist, though I felt this would be the first part of the long process destined ahead. I arrived at his office in Belsize Park and he dressed like an old professor. He listened and then said, "I think I can help you to stay as a man."

I was so angry and he could see I looked shocked. I raised my voice and remember saying, "No, thank you."

I called my GP and arranged a meeting. I took along information and contact numbers about where I should go in order to speed up this transition. Finally I was booked to visit a psychiatrist at a mental health clinic a week later. Before this visit I went to view my new flat in Southwark in London, on a freezing November day. My housing coordinator opened the door to the flat and made my heart stop. This flat (Peabody Estate, Block E, Southwark Street, SE1 2BT) was located at the back of the first floor in an old Victorian complex. It was horrid. It had concrete flooring with men's fitness weights and a pained yellow morel on one of the walls. The next day Michelle drove me there with my things and brought paint with us. I thought that I reached a real low. Michelle couldn't wait to leave and pulled the door behind. I stood there freezing in silent shock and saw her from the window walking to the car. I didn't want her to leave. My Michelle had now actually gone. I stood still for ages in pain, cried my eyes out and made myself sleep.

Then it was time to go and face the psychiatrist alone. I arrived in my black 525e BMW with black out windows and sat for ages wearing my girls tracksuit. I had my

114

thoughts and nerves together and walked into the reception confidently. I waited with some other patients who were sadly there with other mental health problems. I was called into a meeting room where there were five people sat with pens and notepads. I listened while they spoke and I knew I had to satisfy them with my words, to put me through to the next stage. I announced I was completely clear in my mind of my wish. "Look, I'm going to be a girl so to save time I hope you will find me a good candidate."

I left feeling happy and knew I'd just have to wait and fingers crossed. But around this time I heard news that about my brother's battle with bipolar. Something he had been suffering from for a very long time. Because of his illness, he would often go missing. My mum called me in tears and asked if I could use my psychic abilities to find his whereabouts. I felt he was near water. Two days later, she called to say some boys noticed a man near a lake in Berkshire sleeping on a bench.

I finally got the news I had been waiting for. I had been successful for reassignment and had been put forward to the gender clinic at Charing Cross Hospital. I went to visit another psychiatrist there and was explained that I would soon have an appointment with a Dr Barret who'd listen to my thoughts and future wishes. I was growing stronger and yet as each day went by, it was hard going about my daily business dressed as a girl with full make-up in Southwark. By day this area was a hustling business area close to the Blue Finn Building that was being built, later to be the new home of IPC who I wrote my column for.

It was a week later when I visited Dr Barret at the gender clinic. I was called to his office and he explained that today would be known (commonly today) as the First Meeting, as you'd have to pass this one to get to the second. His nature was to come across as quite hard yet he would see me in a further six months and guided me through the process of legally change my name and live as a women for two years.

I felt I had been pushing the envelope far longer. But I think I needed the process to be long after the saddest news reached me. My mother called me quite calmly and simply said "He's gone."

"What, what?"

"Giles. He's passed away."

I was full of shock, in pain and angered. I was told he had suffered a heart attack though, being a psychic, I wanted to look into the real situation. I felt that he had not been assisted in the last hours in his flat. The funeral was arranged and I was going have to find more bravery to attend dressed as a girl.

Chapter 13 — New Alphabet

Choosing my new name seemed to arrive quite easily. I loved America and a name that was always embedded in me was 'JENNA'. I remember President Bush introducing his family on stage at an election campaign for his second term in office, in front of the world media. The name sounded so nice, so strong so American, although I heard the name 'Jenna' derives from Arabic origin Jena, the guardian of the Deadhouse in Malaz City. Someone who has been through the dogs but got herself back up through her own CODES. I had also always loved the all American Desert Blonde glamour look. Porn star Jenna Jameson had always been a fascination, as well as film icon Brigitte Bardot.

Jenna it was, but I needed a new surname. I decided I did not want to keep my old family name so not to hurt anyone. The new surname choice had to come to my new life without any emotions of the old. I always loved the girl's name Leigh and it was the name of a girl (Leigh Jackson) I fancied years before from Brigidine Convent in Windsor. Also, my connection with Native America, and seeing a Red Indian mounted on a horse years before as a spirit in Windsor Great Park was to affirm my last name. I had seen this spirit who pointed to the ground where I found a red stone for which I heard him say "I name you this." His name, he called, was Green Star — a very old rugged man. 'Raine' was native and a name I loved and noticed in print a lot in the back of Tatler Magazine underneath a group picture. Jenna Leigh-Raine was my new name. I kept the circumflex between Leigh and Raine in keeping with my old double-barrelled former name.

My mother seemed a bit upset when I announced I changed my name completely and took her a while to even say 'J'. In time she grew to accept and I loved her more for it. She went from saying J to Jen to JENNA over a year. I singed the legal papers a few weeks before and it felt so right and more real when my legal change documents arrived.

Though, more on our minds was the funeral of Giles. Outside Windsor, I arrived so nervous and mourning for my brother at the same time. Michelle came with me and saw my grief. She walked next to me, side-by-side and grabbed my hand. She was always strong and didn't care what anyone's reaction might be about my change in appearance. Giles was buried in a lovely garden cemetery and his favourite song by U2, *One*, was played from a cassette player.

It was a beautiful funeral, considering. His three children were there, so strong. Mum kept her emotions in too as she accommodated her grandchildren and some of Giles's old mates.

Me in 1996; (right) I was part of a Dazed photoshoot in 2005

Below: New Year's with Johnny Male and Michelle at Sky Hotel.
Above was me at Gwen Stefani's home in Hollywood with
Michelle, Saff (Republica) and Fast from Fun Lovin' Criminals

In the spring of 2007 I was put forward for my gender reassignment surgery to become a full woman. This was during the same year I found a job as an assistant to a lovely American couple, Bill and Kate, in Kensington where

Michelle was a PA. I started firstly as their as dog walker to a beautiful German pointer called Daz. I met Bill and Kate a year before when doing a psychic reading for Kate. They had just moved into a gorgeous, big house in Kensington originally once owned by the Queen's fashion designer Hardy Amies who also designed the costumes to the *2001: A Space Odyssey* movie.

Kate noticed I was stressed about becoming a girl with buck front teeth. Michelle told me Kate asked her to get quotes for corrective work. A couple of weeks later, in June, I began many visits for impressions extrusions and filings in preparation for veneers and a bridge. These operations were painful and bloody but I knew it was going to be so worth it. By the time I completed all my teeth operations, I was amazed. Dr Hayder gave me a gorgeous Californian smile I dreamt of for twenty years.

Now showing off my whitest teeth, it was soon time for my impending GRS surgery on October 13. Michelle, myself, Richard and Rebecca Price, who worked as the dental receptionist I attended and now friends, sat at a café near Kate's on the day I was due to head to the hospital for my operation the following day.

I started a diary following my operation, which went like this. "Putting my bag on my bed the next morning at noon I'm wheeled out on my bed drifting past the strong smell of coffee and baked cakes as I'm wheeled to the elevator up to theatre on the 14th floor. Met there by a nurse checking my details and asking if I could tell him my date of birth, and so forth. I'm not afraid of needles but don't like them either as I thought I had maybe seen these worst months before at my GP's office. You see, I had to have four shots of Volotex which was injected into my abdomen."

"Finally in the anaesthesia room where all life is kept outside and no taxman can find me here. Good vain, needle goes in, sickness treatment injected then the 'White Milk 10 9 8 7 6 5 4 3 2 1. Goodbye Jolyon."

Three hours later — "Jenna, Jenna, it's all over wake up." Now the strangest thing, back in my room 'E', looking at the girl opposite me who had her op at 9am is sitting up eating rice pudding as though nothing happened, wow. This seemed a recurring theme as if we finally put right what was incorrect in the first place.

The rest of the week got uncomfortable as for the long days and endless sleeping due to the anaesthetic. Finally when Friday and Saturday arrived, I had the strangest physical feeling I had ever gone through in my entire life. On the Friday I felt I was being painted with sand inside and had glued cotton inside, then the following day, a continuing piece of thread being picked in one go that lasted thirty seconds. Some girls cry or scream, from others who have this treatment are silent and regardless, you feel for one another.

Dilation began almost straight away and it was painful and repeated twice a day. This would become routine for the rest of my life while continually sexually active. It then quickly became home day and I was allowed to have a much wanted shower after breakfast then more waiting for our nurses to hand out my meds. My blood pressure was checked for the last time and had a final lie down, waiting until a friend or family member to take me home. It was a rare scene for a loved one to pick someone from my position up. I was lucky to have plenty of them, and had people support me through these times. Johnny and my other Republica mates were still in touch and though I hadn't seen Siobhan for years, she knew I was going through this transition and approved of it.

The long goodbyes to the other patients and staff started and I would always remember all the nurses for the rest of my life. The surgery went well though I caught an infection which was to lead to three years of further corrective cosmetic surgeries until the autumn 2012.

Before GRS, I saved up and one Sunday, due to a cancellation, was offered a consolation deal for a hair transplant operation by Dr May of The London Welbeck Hospital. It was an eight hour long process where firstly, your head is injected with anaesthetic, then a long section of skin cut from the nape and then the gap stitched together. The slither of skin with the hair was passed the team of ladies who, under microscope, cut and separate each hair from the core. The area of your hair line, which was already marked for surgery, was drilled one-by-one. I couldn't feel anything apart from a cold sensation from the back of my head where I had been sown up. There were lots of visits to the toilet due to the medications follow.

After lunch, all the hairs were ready for transplanting had been carefully chosen to eventually give a natural appearance. This took hours, but after the eight hours, a powder was sprinkled over the area and the process was over. I then placed my baseball cap over, thanked everyone and went home.

Over the next months, all the visual transplanted hair would naturally drop off apart from the root which later started to appear and grow through. The results were amazing and it was the best money I had ever spent. I've revisited the clinic for reviews since and have kept in touch with a couple of nurses.

On January 30th, 2008, three months after my main op, I returned to Charing Cross. I remember how much snow we had then but I managed to go there for my boob job. I was so excited. The only problem was that the implants I wanted had not arrived. I remember hearing that they would have to be re-ordered that day. Here I was imagining a man on a motorbike delivering my new boobs up the freeway.

Liz Dex, who later was my GRS corrective surgeon, was originally going to do my boobs but due to schedule and the order issue, she could not do it. The next morning however. I was wheeled off the anaesthetic room and needle went in — here we go. I woke up with a shocking beige strap over me but, I didn't care — my new friends, 36DD, arrived. The strap eventually cut and replaced as it was too tight. Surgeon Dr Lada did my op. She was great and sent me home time the following morning. That next day was of the snowiest and my friend Kim Digmon picked me up. We drove skidding down Kings Road in her car to Marks & Spencer store to buy my very first sports bra.

Following that operation, I had my tracheal shave and voice pitch operation. I had the same routine — needle in, and so on. But this turned out to be the most emotional operation of all. The world seemed near but far as I could not speak for around two weeks as my voice box was remapping. I heard crackles at first which would develop into my new voice. I carried with me a small writing pad everywhere I went, saying, "I CAN'T SPEAK. HAD OPERTAION ON MY VOICE; Can I have a tall skinny double shot mocha, please?" Eventually I could hear a smoother much higher pitched version of my voice. I started practising my voice over and over "Hi, I'm Jenna Leigh-Raine." Weeks later, I visited my original voice coach Cristella at Charing Cross and she too was very happy with my results.

My hospital bed, Charing Cross, London following GRS

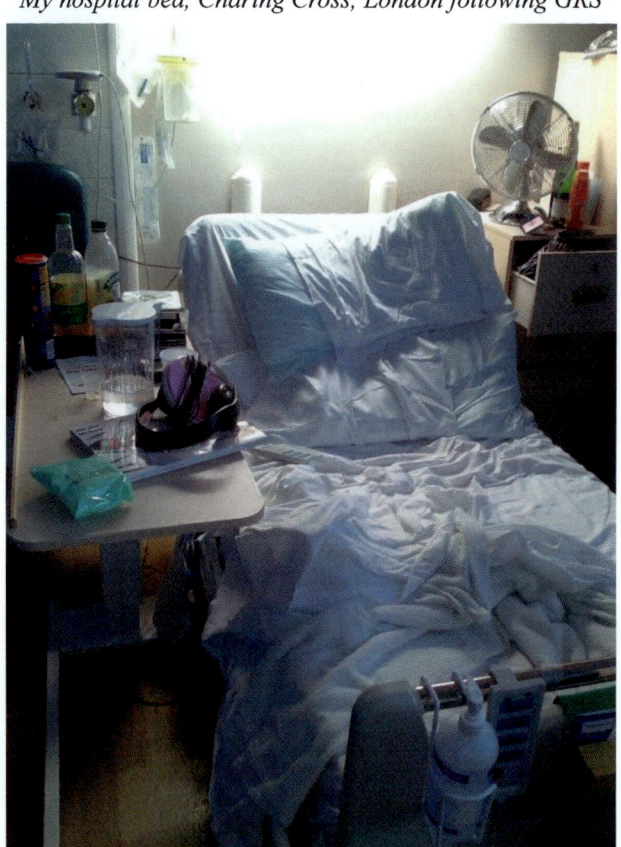

Me in my healing gear at Nelson's with Suzannah and Layla.

MY OLD DIARY ENTRY

August 15th, 2007:

A lot has been going on since my last entry. My brother is getting more ill from his bipolar and mum fears the worse but has learnt to take it day by day

I did another gig last week it went better than expected, been a while. Well I've been doing this so long I should be able to deal with any technical problems should they occur.

August 27th, 2007:

Been such a strange time. I seem to always have some fair-weather friends and noticing more disappear due to my new role as Jenna. It's been years since I started my transition but why do they seem to be able to abandon me with such ease?

Recordings to complete for:

- *New album Dreams In Flatline 2009*
- *Dark Lolita*
- *Sensy-Tiv*
- *Newpornchic*
- *Raised(Genes)*
- *Raine*
- *Losing Faith (may change title to' Dirty Hazard Hate)*

November 12th, 2007:

Had break down after such a build-up of stuff and hearing my brother has gone missing again

He got ill 7 years ago with depression, alcoholism and bipolar .... At the gender centre today I breakdown. I just cracked' about having to hold 'so much together', and waiting so long to have corrective GRS surgery ....One good thing came of this, the gender nurse Iffy and my electrologist Sara ran to console me. Sara, who I am close to, said if is there nothing you can do get her seen quicker?.... Dr Thomas had refused to offer his further assistance but said he would arrange for me to see Cosmetic surgeon Liz Dex for reconstructive surgery.

126

February 28th, 2008:

My ex-girlfriend announced she's met a new guy a lawyer ohhnooooo. This marks the end of an era but I'm so hurt and I'm crying with my tears falling on to 20 pound notes from some job.

March 3rd, 2008:

I heard my brother passed away from a heart attack ...this line written one week after I heard on top of this I have to attend my last assessment in-front of the psychiatrist and pass to get my GRS surgery. My God I've got to hold it all together.

November 5th, 2008:

3 weeks ago I had my gender operation. I feel calm. Dazzle dies yesterday and my job too. Now what? December 3rd, 2008: Last two weeks too much lost my job, dazzle gone, and I even think I touched the Dark Side Back to recording the album.

June 7th, 2009:

Writing this entry in hospital after my reconstructive surgery with pillow between my knees....I remember saying to the surgeon 'what's the holdup why am I waiting so long to go in...Jenna you just had it ...and I said What?!

Day after surgery I crawl up to take a maths test to in order to get my H1/H2 exam, in order to get a job as an assistant nurse.... yeah crazy I know. I've been hanging out here far too long maybe.

August 26th, 2009:

Well I'm lying here trying not to speak after my tracheal shave and pitch voice operation. This has been the most emotional operation. I've got a note book to write messages with for two weeks. "May I have a mocha? With extra shot sorry can't speak."

I even delivered a psychic reading today without talking just writing notes in my book and showing them ....ha-ha.

Soon after my main operation, my job with Kate and Bill ended, and I was struggling but nowhere near like previous times. I was a girl, a musician, a columnist now living in Sloane Square yet poor, cello taping things together month-by-month somehow. I built up such survival tactics. I remember one long standing memory was walking three miles from Old Windsor to Hack and Slash hairdresser in 1990 to ask Stewart Armotrading to lend me 12 pence as I had the rest to afford a mailing stamp to send off a job application form. Knowing this connected me to something bigger.

Chapter 14 — Book of Giles

When we were kids, and because we experienced travelling and being schooled in Rio, Giles and I were often seen as unique. We spoke a mix of languages including Portuguese, and attended a school full of kids speaking Spanish and American English. Our own accents, when we arrived eight years later in London caused us problems. But back at home we found our shared passion in bikes — building them, changing and racing them brought us closer. That was only until his new group of friends left me feeling left out.

He loved to also build replica planes out of balsa wood, stretch material and glue sheets of canvas for wings.

He loved music and his obsession maybe too also be a rock star began early. One of my fondest memories with him was when he got us tickets to see The Cure in Wembley Arena.

We always had to share a room and being three years apart, at times, caused arguments. This was especially the case when we moved to Old Windsor where we debated about what bands and posters we should have on our walls. Despite loving The Cure, we did have opposing views in music.

We went through some hurtful times too. Having grown up in Rio, we watched and listened to terrible arguments between Herbie and mum from top of the stairs. My memories do jump as we lived in many places between 1976 and 86.

I believe that Giles tried to protect me from situations and facts, which I learnt prior to his death. Our natural father, Jon, was never a dad to us, ever. He was more a man-at-odds and I think when he turned up by complete surprise when I was 16 and Giles 19, really affected him in the long-term.

I knew when Giles became a dad for the first time with his partner Georgina, he wanted to tell Jon though sadly he didn't appear at all interested in our lives after his random entrance.

Professionally, Giles became a chef and a very good one too, after attending Slough College to complete a relative course there.

I loved my brother although we did have some almighty rows as we grew from boys to teens to young adults. I suppose it was because we held on tight together as kids. In the UK, we were foreign, and were about to experience a bumpy time whenever we were 'home'. He was more academic than myself, more artistic and musical yet, tragically, a loner. He a participated in everything and was into mechanical interests, music and girls.

Music was our gel. We both loved music and although he introduced me to bands and artists including Gary Numan, he loved Pink Floyd, U2 and, of course, his favourite, The Cure.

His funeral was the most difficult to take. It wasn't just because I lost my brother, but that I would be attending as a woman and I had no idea whether he'd be proud of my new life direction as both of our paths went to different directions.

Following his passing, there were many times where I felt lost so lost and could not keep myself from crying. Yet, I kept strong for my mum whose loss was massive. I worried about her a lot as I noticed she seemed very low and remote, and I did all I could by listening and advising.

Many months after his passing, one evening, I had a visitation and knew it was him. I was shocked to be honest, as he was noisy and I wept so much, mum said out loud while on the phone to me, "Giles don't frighten your sister." This was one of many visits as a couple of my friends told me of occurrences where Giles made a connection with them. His death allowed me to move emotionally closer with my mum, more than I had in many years when we, overtime, grew apart and wishing we had more fab memories like we did in Rio.

Now, in 2009, work was an area which was far more difficult for any 'girl in my situation'. I was pretty and convincing as a female and understood men inside and out. Though, after sometime, my memories of male thought patterns were gone. I didn't really find men easily attractive but recalled their bravado, egos, smell and vulnerabilities. I did start to date guys to see how this would all sit with me. I mean by this time in my life, I had done so much and survived so much, but this was about to prove the hardest hurdle as when it came to going out with a guy, it was so strange and alien. I liked the attention and being spoilt, but I thought with my head past and future, would I prefer to date a guy or a girl?

Chapter 15 — Afterlife

My change of looks attracted a new squad and fellow girl musicians entered my life. They were my rock bitches. Hazel, known as Aze Corleone, Sarah White, and Georgina Baillie from then band MariaMaria produced by Richard James Burgess, of 80s group Living in a Box fame. Maria later disbanded in true rock pomp. Georgina later went on to sing backup for 80s star Adam Ant and was dealing with her own press issues, being the granddaughter of Fawlty Towers star Andrew Sachs in the middle of that famous media storm involving Jonathan Ross and Russell Brand's public prank call to Andrew about her.

It was the summer of 2009 and I met the new Guns N' Roses members thanks to Georgina who sent me a text asking me if I wanted to join them at the Met Bar in Park Lane, London during their appearances at the Reading Festival. It was great meeting then lead guitarist of Guns N' Roses, DJ Ashba, he was a true, looking rock star and was one of the greatest musicians at the time. Axl Rose wouldn't be pulled from his hotel room at 3am after Georgina and I just got back from taking the boys on the most surreal night out to some top rock venues in Soho. The kids couldn't believe who and what they were seeing. I said at the door of one venue, "Hey guys, I'll do the talking… Hi, umm, right. I've got Guns N' Roses with me and I'm gonna need a table and a lot of Jack Daniels." The manager of that venue didn't believe me so I asked her to come to the car. "How many tables do you want," she replied. It was so surreal yet so true.

Three months later they returned and we hang together, Ron 'Bumblefoot' was one of the nicest guy in rock that I ever met and DJ was still looking as cool as.

Soon I was working again for another American family looking after their two pups and stayed in their home whenever they were out of town. These jobs were hard to find but my previous reference via a call to New York City, I heard went a long way. They were a lovely couple who worked in law and finance — Mary Breize and husband Cris from the Big Apple. I found myself sitting in the grand sitting room thinking that it would be one more year until the thirty year landmark since I wrote *3Dlove* (my first ever track) — almost thirty years since I made my first prediction and by February 2011, ten years since I started my column. I was coming in very full circle.

I later started to volunteer at The Royal Hospital, Chelsea down the road from my home. I spent my time sitting, listening and chatting to troops from the Wars. Hearing all their memories I shall always remember. Fitz, almost a hundred years young, the oldest Vet at that time, and George were sweet gents. I remained there for about six months until I had a new calling about my music.

A new two-track single called *Alternation*, later renamed *HUMANWAY*, about always changing, which included the line 'She Is Rock star'. It was a phrase to say 'all she is, done, survived. Another track, *Actress*, about darker things who I wrote the lyric (alternative version) with, and partially about, close friend Lorna Bliss, also a Britney Spears impersonator.

January 23rd, 2011

It's done and I feel calm ...my friend Lorna is on her way over and I'll have to explain why that Diet Coke she's got with her will taste oh so good next years when it will be champagne.

Bye jenna x

May 20th, 2011

Last night, my comeback into modelling, I was invited to attend the BENDOVER porn disco, many photographs and now I'm DAKOTA. Model, actress, musician, columnist, and it was a fun night where fans of some of the UK's well-known adult actresses made an appearance and photographed by press and fans. I meet that evening Paige Foxx — porn star and the sweetest little pocket rocker. Her sister is there too and we jump and pose around in a hot tub under lights for the cameras. I also saw Dave Tubs (Professor Tubs) as he is known. We met at the 2010 Erotica fair in Olympia London where we spoke about how he could assist my modelling career. He was a gent with a naughty smile who lived in Bracknell, Ascot near where my brother's life had ended. We spoke and he later asked me to come to this Playboy event. He and his friend picked me up from my house and we drove to the venue close to London Bridge. This week also had a serious side. I must get my head on and tune my guitar ready to possibly rehearse a set with Swedish pop star Therese.

Later that week...

Last Saturday at the porn disco I met some great new friends. "Cherry", a gorgeous brunette with eyes of Jenna

Jameson and face of Cheryl Cole. Eva May model from Bluebird TV named Giggles by myself was also there.

That following Thursday saw the reality of who I was then came running to get me again as I would be 'In stitches' once again due to another reconstructive review. Weeks later after this operation I woke from surgery not recalling much but taken to Recovery at the Riverside ward where I had my first GRS surgery three-and-a-half-years before. I saw all the old faces and joked that maybe I could the same job as them myself by that point.

Chapter 16 — In Orbit

August 2011 was a long month as I took part in rehearsals as part of a band called Kalkulus. We were made up of three with founder member Karl Heard leading the pack. One of our bigger gigs was when we supported 90s dance legends Orbital. Our performance was during the week of the London riots in Brixton, not that far from the venue we were due to appear. At the time, I was not in the right mood for performing. I was on automatic, but was not bothered just playing the rock star. I knew my parts — I was drummer, guitarist and keyboardist. There was a lot to do but I could do it.

By the time we were halfway through, the set the place was rammed. It was a good gig but it reminded me of what I didn't like about all this anymore. "If I was ever gonna do this again," I said in rage to myself, "It will not be at midnight, without crew or techies."

The band had a few internal eruptions. Karl, who was fronting this outfit, was dealing with his own demons which I felt psychically. During his hard times, I was always there for him. We dated on-and-off for a while but I just didn't seem ready for a committed relationship.

Chapter 17 — Do or Die

During this July / August 2011 period, I was embarking back into glamour modelling through friend and porn producer, Dave Tubbs. We became close. Earlier that year, in March, I had my battles in court to remain in my Sloane Square property due to lease issues. When push came to shove, I finally left there and went to stay with Dave in Bracknell (the town God forgot to dismantle). I was lost here. It was a million roads and years back from where I had been. I'd already done with chasing up and down the foot hills with rock stars. Bracknell was a huge challenge.

Dave was easy going and understood different situations so well and he could see I felt a little lost. One morning, while walking to catch the long coach ride back into London, I found myself so down. As I walked through a late 70s underpass, covered in old images of folk, it reminded me too much of my dark teenage years. It triggered a terrible panic attack. My God, I've done so much in my life, been to Hollywood a hundred times, why am I here? What has happened? I was in severe pain.

I rarely left Dave's house rarely but when I did go out, he'd set up a meet-and-greet system for me to meet fans of his. This period did serve a purpose and Cherokee, my cat, got to feel grass and got along with Dave's own cats. I also went with Dave and his friend Matt to Birmingham for an event at the NEC for the adult industry. We made this in a two day road trip and stayed at this rather low-end hotel in Aston. When I returned into my own flat in Sloane Square, I sensed that despite a difficult summer, things were starting to come together, which would always be a mystery as to how I reached that turnaround but I thought the spirits were by my side so, thank you Giles!

Chapter 18 — Where Angels Fear

Upon my return to London after that summer, I realised I had changed, more than I knew, and could possibly have realised. Back at my old flat, recently renovated with the new smell of carpet and paint hid corners old. I'd worked in and around the adult industry for a while, and it was not as bad as you may anticipate. It became easier and I knew all the steps to undertake the bigger projects in short deadlines. One Saturday afternoon, while walking up Kings Road, I received a call from a lady called Steph asking if I were available to work that night — I had a reputation and was in demand.

But my time in the adult industry was a little bitty as the months went by. That autumn was my gender corrective operation number seven — that's if you discount all the other operations I had over the past five years, now equalling 14. Each time I was wheeled into the anaesthetic room, almost felt a break and an escape. Now leave me alone everyone, I thought. Sometimes, I felt excited here and I knew the faces of quite a few nurses by then. We banter — "Meeting you here again," we'd say.

The anaesthetics and the thought of being out of the world was an appealing thought. It meant I was 'switched off', no problems could get me here. However, I woke up after this particular operation slightly disappointed, as though the sleep was never quite long enough. This operation was to improve what had been ruined four years before but safely now in the hands of plastic surgeon Liz Dex.

Each Tuesday for two years after, I visited the gender clinic next to the hospital. I would look forward to go there mainly to see Sara (treating me for facial electrolysis). I told her more about my life than I did with any psychiatrist before. She knew everything. All my dramas and fights to survive. Electrolysis was the most painful procedure out of all the gender procedures but I felt it was worth it.

Back in the anaesthetic room, I jest that I could break my record to be 'Out'. The milk was sent into my stream and, by the tenth second, I was smiling about still being there as I fell asleep. I think the record for the anaesthetic to affect me was 13 seconds, but it still gave me time to embrace the surgeons' last words, "Relax, Jenna and see you later."

Soon after the operation and back in my flat again, I received a call from Dave Tubbs, asking if I wanted to make some cash, and if so Paige Fox would be contacting me. Paige to this day is a close friend. She makes me laugh every time we meet and was also a survivor, I could tell. She was petite yet perfectly formed, and sexy as hell. Almost everywhere she went, Nelson, her little white duke Jack Russell followed.

On the phone, Paige invited me to a hen do of another model called Kaz-B. Paige and Kaz went towards their own paths and worked as porn actresses and escorts. "Be at Stanton station in Dorset," said Kaz where I'd be greeted by her boyfriend and agent JJ who would take me to the venue. Kaz too was a small bundle of fun and instantly, we clicked and it was just as well we did, as afterwards we would be performing together a live strip and girl-on-girl show.

The do itself was actually, really wild and fun evening — like a scene from an American movie. The house they had rented was located in the most hidden reaches of the Dorset Hills. Through the deep fog, we held on tight as we glided up the tiny hilly roads, laughing and arrived late but alive. I had noticed horses inside an oval wood building, the house turned out to be owned by a top trainer. Later in the night, we sat, looking up at stars, drinking champagne in the hot tub. It was all fine and dandy.

Despite enjoying the adult industry lifestyle, I had to be careful of my reputation. In the age of Facebook, where all your life and private detail are advertised and scrutinised. I had two accounts; one under my real name and the other as Dakota, for my modelling work. It didn't take long to discover this was a bad idea. I have nieces and I was getting worried about the more I forged into the modelling, the sooner it became obvious I could hardly keep this world apart from my family life. I realised most of my close friends knew my other work and were completely supportive about it. "Who cares, you're a survivor and why should you have to worry?" one would say.

The reasons for my reservations was because I was getting more interest from model agents wanting to shoot me. I had not been in this sort of demand since I started modelling at 17. I needed to take them though — since moving back to my flat, it was becoming more difficult to handle financial matters. I needed quick cash and these photo shoots helped. One I fondly recall was when I spent a day with highly experienced model and mate, Nikkita. It was a fun shoot in Battersea, where we were shot by a big film producer. These were big jobs.

Chapter 19 — Paigehood

Paige and I had such an incredible bond and she helped me through the battles from the autumn of 2011. She was such a giggly, lovely Croydon girl who was fostered through tough times. She was as kind as you would expect. She had the biggest, bright eyes and hadn't lost that touch of youth and expectancy. I believed no-one had come to pick her up from school either! I felt connected to Paige and loved her as a person — she loved cooking and Nelson, her little Jack Russell was family. Her sister, May, a teenager then looked so much like Carolyn Jones from the Elvis film King Creole — I was convinced May was Carolyn in her former life. She was a seventeen year old, wild rockabilly girl with sharp black fringed hair and had almost oriental eyes. She sang to me once in Berkeley Square on Paige's birthday.

I was involved in a family that made me feel secure and forget the past — I couldn't rate them highly enough. I was surely and finally 'Starting to Forget' about my past, a romantic term I felt for losing, moving and changing.

My life was becoming so different, a contrast to my past that could barely remember, which made me happy. Life was now better. You could notice the transformation from the inside and out, yet even with all those hormones blasted into my system daily (and for the rest of my life), I still found myself sexually attracted to girls. I liked the attention a guy would show me, don't get me wrong, but I was careful and aware in case a client would turn on me. I was always vigilant for my own security and gender, the past still played on the back of my mind, despite the improvement to my situation.

Chapter 20 — Babes in the Wood

The only moments of my past which I can truly look back fondly were those hazy summer beach days in LA where I was flying and existing under the radar. I remember in 1998 when a client, and almost Julianne Moore lookalike called to book an appointment for a reading. Her apartment was two blocks from Sunset Boulevard, and one down from Melrose and I was there a week after her reading for a party she invited me to. This was around the time Republica had visited and after I performed my track Nebulablue on TV. She found me when I was working as for a psychic phone line company called Twin Vision American, second largest company of its kind to Psychic Friends Network, which Dionne Warwick was the face of. The company was based in Malibu where, when I left home for the UK, owner Jeffrey Powers set up a satellite system just so clients could still get hold of me via my cell phone. I could be walking through Notting Hill and my phone would call asking if I would read someone in Texas or other.

I worked there from 1998 to around 2008 on many, many of these lines. One day, back in my home in Sloane Square, ten minutes after taking a similar call I pulled the phone from the socket and put it in the bin, I just could not listen anymore. I needed a break from after a decade of these calls and anything psychic-related. Amy Schofield, who had been one of the receptionists there used to call and ask, with sensitivity, if I could just take one more call before I go to bed at 2am.

But heading close to 2012, it was a long time since I'd moved on from working at this call centre, I had a call from

Amy out of the blue. Having been in touch during my gender operations, she knew the new me. The call took me by huge surprise as I was shocked by how she remembered me after all that time. As our talk went on, she told me she was now working for a UK-based TV company which owned both Psychic Today and Babestation. It was funny because just two weeks before, I had been in Birmingham at Kaz-B's home modelling through her webcam when her then boyfriend, a dab hand at techy things, ran in to say, "Jenna, Babestation have just emailed, asking if you would like to audition for them."

I explained to Amy that I was just not interested in phone work at all anymore, and just could not do it. Babestation however sounded more appealing than Psychic Today. Me on Babestation, and after all the pain I had been through with operations, I looked and felt the part.

However, what happened next remained a mystery. I told Amy I'd do the TV show but not the home phone service. I sent off my details and application to Babestation on the day of my other audition for Psychic Today. I was told how both stations' managers joked about which channel I would end up going to. At my audition for Babestation, a runner was sent to meet me in the waiting area, though I didn't see anyone. Finally, the boss for Psychic Today came to the waiting room and asked for me.

Psychic Today boss, Sarah Cherry was a beautiful brunette who I followed up the stairs to be greeted and introduced by the team. I'd then display my ability, again making one girl run and cry — sorry, I'm a real medium. The pitch went well because the day later, I got the job to work for them though yet, I wished it had been from Babestation.

On my first day with Psychic Today, I made it to the studio floor just below Babestation where I recognised and bumped into a few old, familiar faces from the adult industry. But I remember the pain I had with my feet. With me, I took my special shoes and boots which travelled with me through so many journeys and troubles, but always saw me through. I always buy then one size too small so they appeared more fitted, cool and feminine. This played hell on my poor feet and years later, now suffered from bad bunions and was due for surgery. This would not be the end of my friendship with morphine and milk propanol.

The morning of my very first show at Psychic Today was on November 24th, 2011. At 6am, I got off the tube at Portland Street. It was very early and I felt a mix of excitement and nerves. I decided to jump into a coffee shop — the only one open in the area at that time, and 500 yards from Cellcast Studio, where Psychic Today was based. I looked at this young, loved up couple in front of me seemingly a bit wasted from the previous evening that turned into the morning.

When I later arrived to the studio, I waited in the green room for others to arrive. I was then briefed by the producer and the show at 9am began, live. I received a welcome by the presenter and then asked if I would like to answer some texts from viewers and all was going well.

The next week was an ease. My psychic strengths seemed visible. Being on Live TV was a breeze on screen and off, and was comfortable enough to reveal my past and who I'd become today. There were some very shocked faces, though more as they didn't realise I wasn't born a girl. Months flew by here and I still had the chance to bump into the girls I knew from Babestation who knew me as

Dakota. I felt a strong connection with them due to my past roles in the adult world. We were good friends and made my desires to work at Babestation that much greater.

The summer of 2012 arrived when our studio was being refitted, and we had to share a tiny, hot studio right next to the Mastiii channel studios in the same building. My time with Psychic Today inspired me to form a new album. I had the idea in my head and whilst working here, I set about inventing new beats and create new songs. I recorded myself singing melodies, sounds and beats with my voice into my phone and carry on with the day.

A personal highlight for me at Psychic Today was forming new real friendships, such as Aldo Raffa, a young psychic who was part of the new breed, and Abi Magauran, a gorgeous blonde presenter full of fun and zest. Us three, and sometimes fellow psychics Tiffany Wardle and Lisa Marie, making the five of us were part of the 'A Team' where we were up for giggles.

Working in a tiny studio made it very difficult for us. With no A/C, our producer Nilesh and presenter Charlotte Partlow, we did our best to hold things together. I don't recall what happened, maybe a mix of the heat, but a highly bizarre voicemail came in and I couldn't hold it together. Then, eight or so minutes of classic TV ensued where Charlotte and I corpse and sweated with laughter.

Another colleague, Abi later that day said she had tickets to a club where some of the gold medal Team GB athletes were attending, and I agreed to go. By this point, I was not really into clubbing anymore after all the years appearing as a glamour model in VIP section and drinking too much Goose Vodka. It was a fun night where Abi and I were towered by a medallist from the rowing crew. That was one of many outings with the guys, as we had countless trips to the pub to ease off the tensions after an odd slow show.

One of the bigger outings we had was on the day of the Queen's Diamond Jubilee, Aldo and I ran through the streets near Chelsea to get a good view wearing our silver plastic tiaras. We took two bottles of champagne and chocolate cake with us but couldn't get close enough as security was everywhere. I said, with my voice so loud to a security guy to let us through, but Aldo went that much further by saying, "Jenna, you don't live here, run." So here I was, jumping over an iron fence, breaching security! I lost Aldo for ten minutes, later finding out he was caught and escorted back out onto the street. But, what a day in history — me, Aldo, champagne, the rain, and the Queen's magic.

My thoughts as the year came close to the end were changing again. I had already done so much in my life, but a sense of boredom waved over me and I wish I could have been given a chance to work at Babestation. As Christmas arrived, I was getting excited about another work party at the famous number 31 Portland Place where *The Kings Speech* movie was filmed.

As New Year approached, I found myself standing on the rooftop of the office garden, looking out to the sky and searching for the next stage in my life. It had to be life fulfilling and must not play safe this time. Although I was finally secure financially and friendships are strong for first time in years, I knew I must go and do what I was aching to do. As January arrived, I sensed change and my shifts were shortened due to a new influx of psychics trying out their skills. Some would be TV savvy enough to survive and others decided the scene didn't suit them and fade. Psychics at work had been mentioning they could see me living back in LA eventually. I particularly like one of the newer members, Simone Murrin Fitzpatrick, who on her first day said to me, "Oh, Jenna, you're my favourite."

I loved my job but I was getting burnt out and had a severe psychic attack, live on TV and signalled to presenter Claire Anstey sitting next to me at the desk that I was in trouble. Only some short weeks later, I was looking for other work, and one morning I had a phone call in my gym in South Kensington. It was Laura Michaels (who starred in my own adult movie years before) from Playboy TV, wondering if I'd be available to come for an audition, which to me was amazing.

On the evening before my audition, I packed my suitcase full of bikinis, makeup and shimmer. Standing, waiting for my train I was slightly nervous yet so excited. The audition itself was in a studio where I had been before. I was here in 2006 when Terry and I came for a meeting with Phil Barry to scout our work, he's now running Playboy TV by this point. I relaxed in their dressing room for a while, and slowly got ready for my debut and audition live on TV. I bumped into Pretti who then channel hopped (which was a common thing in Babe TV culture) coming from Babestation and now at Playboy, so I had a good chance to catch up with her before I was due to go on at 9pm.

The show started at 9pm on the dot, and I say to camera, "Hello boys and girls, I'm Dakota. Welcome to my first evening here on Redlight channel 886, I hope you're all gonna phone in and get involved." For that all night shift at least I'm now a babe. I've been a psychic and presenter for the last year or so, but now I'm a babe in the wood, whatever happens.

But troubles were ahead, as per my psychic shock just weeks before. The days that followed were quite heart-breaking as my Psychic bosses were shocked and disappointed I had not informed them of my initial plans, though I mentioned the day I arrived in November 2011 that I was here to enter the modelling world. But their upset affected me when, on Monday the January 18th, 2013, I couldn't get out of bed for the next two days distraught and hurt. Three days later, I put on my thinking cap and called up model agency owner Phil Green and explained my predicament. He said he think he could get me back onto another babe channel, and would give me a call the next day.

Meanwhile, I arranged to meet up with a beautiful mate of mine, Jaz who at this point was still working at Babestation for the Mastiii channel. We caught up at the Hard Rock Cafe around the corner from The Playboy Club in Mayfair where she was working part time. We had a few laughs down memory lane and walked her to the door at Playboy then made my way past The Metropolitan Hotel where I drank shots with Guns N' Roses years before.

By then Phil put me onto someone who later became my PR agent and new opportunities would open for me. There were lots of media interest in my life story and many weeks later I was featured inside *The Star on Sunday* newspaper.

Mobile phone diary and notes to myself

Told off at work, bed by 4pm can't think or breathe
Week of feb [sic] 27 tomo giles [sic] 5th anniversary
passing and me and paige [sic] will work
Karl sending love texts and I'm broke til 10th march, and
foot operation fri [sic]
Seeing surgeon Dex again need more revision
Rehearseals [sic] for DIRTY Machine summer gig
Febuary [sic] 2012 marks the 30th anniversary to which
it seemed I wrote my first lyrics to 3D-Love
Survival tactics
You will need selotape [sic]/water/stamps/shoes

Since becoming Jenna, I dedicated part of my life to modelling and boxing. Bottom picture credit: Joe Cordwell, in Folkestone, 2013.

Picture credit: Sanjay Kaŕki near Paradise Cove, CA, 2015.

This is me on Chat Girl TV in the same building as Playboy. I also worked at Redlight TV.

This is me presenting on Psychic TV, 2012.

Pictured here with the girls' team at City Warriors Boxing, London, 2015.

Chapter 21 — Fight Song

In 2002, I was approached by Channel 5 in the UK to be featured on a celebrity based show called 'Exclusive'. They filmed and interviewed me around Kensington about my then psychic life in-and-out of LA. Almost a decade on I had been on many shows and preferred the setting of presenting or being featured, it was a media I knew.

Having that presenting experience helped me get the offers I craved. In the summer of 2012 for example, I was contacted about yet another pilot for a psychic focused programme, showcasing psychics from around the UK. I filmed my part at Limehouse studios inside a recording suite of which ex-indie front man Pete Doherty of Babyshambles was recording a day before. This studio happened to be an inch from where I recorded my track *Domination* for Richard Norris and Andy Chatterly's album in 2005. They wanted to show me in my preferred surroundings and I began, once the lighting was in place, to read the interviewer doubling as producer. It was all going well and my friend Abi Magauran from Psychic Today came along for support. She also enjoyed to help carry my slightly heavy and beloved black Gibson copy electric guitar as signed by Gary Numan. After being filmed, Abi decided to get a well-deserved drink by the Tower of London riverside on a sunny yet chilly, perfect day.

Shortly after that, another TV offer came in and this time it was for a planned series, where a team of psychics and ghost hunters were summoned. Driven to a castle setting in the country, I knew I was going to this on a bad note as I seemed disjointed in my interest as a psychic. I was playing the 'reluctant medium' again, music was more in my mind. I dressed that day more rock chick and just delivered. The lovely Katie Keeley, who also worked on Psychic Today, was present. I loved her, she was the most fun you could wish for. Like me, she was a rebel and were like kids during lunch. As part of this programme, I was interviewed where I explained my methods of work as a psychic.

The day in this castle was a long one. After lunch, we were asked to sit in one area and see if we could pick up on any feelings from the grounds. We were then asked to read one another briefly in what I'd like to call a 'Power Reading'. The producer of this show, Simon Ludgate, seemed impressed enough with me and after all the other psychics and hunters performed their piece to camera we were then escorted back to the train station.

On the ride home, I settled into my seat and watched probably my favourite film to date on my tablet. The movie, The Runaways starring Kristen Stewart, who played the part of 70s rock icon Joan Jett. It almost changed me inside, I connected with everything about it. A rebel who knew what she wanted, a musician who played electric guitars, loud. By definition, this was a key moment, and fuelled me, and in the weeks that followed I set out completing my newest album. *Onyx* the album was about someone who went into dark places to collect those who were lost. This album was the hardest I ever worked on, but I produced and recorded it myself in my studio like normal. I loved it and felt it was a true backdrop to my life and recorded a dark instrumental for the opening track, *In Stitches*.

A month or so later, a friend who was staying with Dave Tubs at the time, mentioned she was about to start work at Chat Girl TV, another Babe channel. I asked her if she would pass on my details, which she did and a week later, I began my first shift. It was a lovely atmosphere there and was based within the head offices of Playboy UK. I prepared myself, dressed and ready, yes I was playing the glamour role again. The boss stood off set just to see me settle in and after I completed my first introduction to camera, said "You're very good at presenting." How flattering, I thought. All my previous experience had come into play and I was happy. They called me back and I returned for my next shift a few days later.

During my time here, Simon was in touch and mentioned he was starting up a new TV channel which was owned and fronted by controversial David Icke. I did not have a good feeling about being associated though was more interested in presenting than being worried about who I was working for. I went for a meeting and joined by a couple of other psychics I met that day filming at the castle.

During that meeting, a psychic off camera said to me "I think you are going to end up living in LA. That's where you are supposed to be and will be happy." Those constant reminders kept me going as that desire never left me. However, I did not return back to the set of this new show and carried on at Chat Girl, where it got more fun, chatting away with the different producers like Krystal Niles.

Then, my life took another turn for the interesting. It must have been only a week after and I was approached to compete in boxing events with City Warrior Boxing (CWB), based near Liverpool Street near where the bankers worked in London. Gary Stasek was the trainer, a quiet, yet lovely man who was a true professional. I had taken up boxing purely for fitness reasons two years earlier due to disinterest with other gym methods. I stopped after six months due to being asked out more than once by fitness trainers. I just wanted to box and get on with it. So when the opportunity with CWB came up, I took it.

I travelled each Tuesday, between my shifts at Chat Girl TV, to the sessions, though knowing nervously I would be very exposed in this arena. Even if Gary could tell of my gender change, he made no real sign. I loved the sessions and a team made of many girls who worked harder in a gym than any of the newbies would ever exercise. This was real boxing and I loved it.

Our first matches was within five months of our first session. We trained hard, properly building our experience and levels to be suited and matched up with someone similar to us. On the evening of our match nerves were everywhere. One-by-one we were called from our dressing room for our fight. My fight was with 27-year-old Stacey Honey'Bee Leighton. I was called first for my big walk out up to the ring passing the audience under spotlight. My entrance tune was *Tainted Love* by Marilyn Manson. We tapped gloves and the bell rang for Round One, there was no getting out of it now. You couldn't imagine how physically gruelling it was, and we went through all three two-minute long rounds. While I annoyingly lost by a point, we hugged each other at the end knowing we've done it — our first fight. It brought with it a feeling you couldn't describe.

Boxing I think saved me. It gave me strength, mental focus and the team of us girls became friends, which when you are fighting for all you have it was sometimes difficult.

I loved it and went on to fight in the Models Fight Night in late 2013. Boxing became my focus, something I took pride in and even trained hard away from the gym.

I had between boxing and Chat Girl, webcam modelling, and writing my column. I even donned a white doctor's coat to give healing to those suffering from cancer, tumour, and pain at Nelsons Pharmacy treatment rooms near Mayfair. I had done so over the last two to three years, including pet healing and by placing my mind, hands, and adding hot energy endeavoured to rid the body of ailments.

Healing was a new and common concept in the holistic world and it would further my ability for a psychic but it isn't for all. It all started in 1996 when my aunt said that I healed our cat as it was thought his leg was broken. I treated people who were in their second to fourth stage of cancer who sought a healer on top of their hospital treatment.

By this point, I marked my 30th anniversary of being a psychic. I must have, in my career, delivered over 60,000 readings. I can't be sure obviously, though when I was 15, I kept a book marking each like a prison wall. I didn't think this day would really have much meaning, though it did. My emotions grew about where my life was and what I truly wanted next. It came through another completely different route.

In 2013, I met a lady called Mathilde who ran a property company in Mayfair that focused on interior and development. We met as friends for lunch often until she asked me to join her team. I had never worked in an office setting as far as I could remember, this was so foreign to me, and after I accepted and started working for her, I sensed Mathilde could tell at times I was drifting. I did my best and learnt over the months but couldn't get used to planning, design, and office culture. I was due soon to take back to the boxing ring and on the night at The Coronet Theatre in Elephant and Castle London, the whole property team surprised me by being there. It was good for me and I dug deep to find maybe some discipline needed to maybe work in a 8am-6pm world.

In late June, while waiting for a girlfriend to meet me in Sloane Square, a rush of people were making their way out of the tube entrance and walked towards where I was waiting. Suddenly finding myself in the middle of the crowd, I was in total shock. In my time, I met or bumped into hundreds of stars, whether through the Brit or Hollywood scene. Here though, I saw myself seeing David Sylvian, famed for his years in 80s band Japan. I couldn't believe it, he was always the one — a true musical composer of ethereal greats. I shouted his name and he stopped. We spoke, and by accident, I said, "David, I've always wanted to meet you. I go to bed listening to your music." Oh dear, I thought — that came out wrong. He raised a little smile at least. As soon as we said our goodbyes, I placed a message on the Facebook fan page for Japan, yet somehow many didn't believe me and the replies went into meltdown.

Sadly, meeting David was the highlight of the summer. That month ended with work in an office where my feeling of any enthusiasm was fading and I wasn't feeling my best. I had been feeling slightly unwell and not sure what was wrong. My GP sent me for blood tests and found out there was a possibly my illness was through bad nutrition through poverty. Perhaps the cheap Raman noodle in LA in 95 was one of many causes.

I suppose the illness was triggered by the lack of self-belief I still had in me. And it always struck me how people would comment about how far I've been at that point. Mathilde made such, in July, while we were together in a cab. "You have changed but you're still a little wild," she observed. I was happy inside and that, in all my 45 years and trials of truth and legend, I was 'still wild'. This again brought my inner-musician in me where I decide it was finally the right moment to begin recording new album material and do it in my adopted home — Los Angeles.

It had been nearly ten years since I was last in LA. Here I was, in May 2015, at Heathrow, boarding at gate 23a to catch my afternoon flight to LAX. Security was much tighter since I was last on the plane and I felt great arriving to my beloved as a WOMAN. The feeling this time was a lot different to where I was when I first went to LA 30 years ago. I was there for discovery back then, I've learnt that I was never going to belong to a convention or routine, rather adapt my own CODES to the Hustle.

The trip to LA did however, burn a hole in my bank account. Debt was a curse of the numbered but I made sure that this wasn't going to affect my time there. Besides, I'd coped penniless in LA before. I remember back in 98 whilst Arjen and I decided our chips were up for a while in that November, and we helped each other get home including another lost bandit. I paid those debts that rose to extortionate levels, but like a bounty hunter, I could see them in my rear view. So trying to get back to LA, considering what I owed at that time, it was an opportunity I had to take. Thankfully, however, I had support from my friends in London that helped me out of that rut.

These particular friends I knew from healing where I'd be able to see into their future in all its fragrance. A lovely old hairdresser, Ivon introduced me to these group of lovely ladies. Rosie, who lived above Ralph Lauren in South Kensington of which her long standing landlord was no other than model Cara Delevingne. Her father, a property mogul, was Rosie's man to go to if a facet was blocked. She a wonderful, wonderful lady who would tell me so many stories about a Flower display artist who worked at St Paul's Cathedral among many other grand London residence.

Rosie came to me via two other ladies — one of which was Claudia Bolter, by now a dear friend I would go and grieve my pains to. She owned C&G hair of Motcomb Street in Knightsbridge which has since closed. In between healing from the world famous Nelson's Pharmacy when not working for Mathilde, I would venture to hear the latest gossip and pour out my struggles and share years of fun with Claudia. Before she sold her salon, she told me six months before that, after my years of helping them and her friends, she wanted to get me a ticket 'Home'.

"I want you to go out there see how it feels after ten years and if it's somewhere you really would want to live in again," Claudia said.

In late April, I was sitting downstairs in the salon with Holly, a beauty technician, who helped to book my flights. So my trip out to LA was a gift from a group of ladies I now called my 'Golden Girls'. I protected them as much as I could in gold light and healing and they helped me do something I thought I could only do alone. Thank you, girls.

The flight was long and not fun. There were around thirty young guys and girls from Ireland on route for some fitness trip. The noise they made was constant. They were loud chatting until I stood up to this one chap. "I'm a trained boxer so if anything's going to go off at 30,000 feet I got it covered." All quiet then prevailed for an hour then off they were again — though I understood their hype. This wasn't their eleventh or twelfth trip 'home' but instead their first taste of Where Angels Come to Sleep. Other than that, it was a bumpy ride, a bit of a let-down which later left me with a huge migraine.

When I landed, the airport's customs changed so much — it was almost as if I had to undress to my bra to make sure I had no concealed weaponry! My friends from Claudia's salon who lived in LA greeted me and we made our way to the streets I knew so well. We pulled over along the way while I said 'hi' to Sunset Boulevard opposite the House of Blues where I had many good memories.

I knew days were going to flash by with the sweetness of LA in my mind. The pink night skies were magical as I planned my fact finding ways for the forthcoming weeks. The Golden Girls may have been thousands of miles away but they helped me touch for the first time with my battled old feet and healing body of many years of operations to the golden sand of Santa Monica. 5, 4, 3, 2, and 1 my feet would touch — I made it. I'm home, I say, smiling. I had come full circle.

The next few weeks followed where I explored my old haunts and apartments which didn't seem to look the same though they were at the right addresses. I even took the bus as, why not! I'd done it in 87 crossing North on Broadway Downtown to use my transfer ticket to catch the next bus to Alhambra to see Crystal and Sandy. But I somehow always felt unstable, in a dangerous place when I was ever in one.

The people hadn't changed there. They are all different but I sensed they were hard workers. I noticed fast that LA had set in place a level of which to start. I felt that also when I observed people in my three bus journeys there.

During this particular bus trip however, I did discover something new — Culver City Westfield mall Target superstore. Every piece of real life LA citizen from the members of the Forces, who got discount at checkout, to the single girl on minimum wage was there. I loved it in a way that said "Jenna, whatever you've been through, we got it all here under one roof — from survival packs to trolleys big enough to put in an engine." The people here were real and I saw the best of LA and also the worst that never recovered from recession.

I managed to arrange to be part of a bikini shoot that took place in the most idyllic patch of Paradise Cove in Ventura County up the road from Malibu. I saw dolphins behind us as I posed. After the shoot, I sat momentarily on the sand taking in everything and more.

I could hardly believe everything that had happened and why everything happened. Am I psychic, a child who grew up to change, what was wrong and show others how to survive and recover, or am I saying goodbye to the past? By the end, I knew I wanted to, one day, settle near paradise but to do that I have to return home one more time to complete unfinished business.

I hated to leave LA but I knew I must. I realised everything that I was scared of from my teens and beyond. I faced the rough, but maybe from here I was just looking to find my place in the world. Find peace with who I am — single and about to be asked to compose and produce music for film. Stunned silence, hands together, rested on knee to face, tear falls a dream down.

I never planned this magical alternative life. All I ever really wanted was to be a musician and for it to be central. But before that maybe put here to help others then my music will play loud'

A year passes over and I'm demoing some punk rock songs. It's true, as I look over the last forty years, and share my birthdate with Mr Sex Pistol himself John Lydon, I realise I've done my very best to be myself. I intend to survive further and be exactly where I want to be – live a #punklife.

Fin

JENNA

HEALING (doctorate)

When you become a psychic medium for many years, your ability rises and develops, and your 'Chip' gets upgraded. For me, this upgrade was the ability to heal. It wasn't that long ago when I noticed that I was able to see illnesses by scanning a person's body whilst they had their back to me. By staring and scanning I was, and am, able to smell, find shadows in colour which I can translate as cancer, tumour, or pain. I am also able to see dietary cure paths and pain relief, mixed by my hand suspended over a patient's body.

This ability to HEAL is one part of being a healer added to mediumship. I can also, via remote viewing, give 'Absent Healing' where I locate my client's in my mind, circling them and pull the ailment, feelings and problem — shielding them, protecting them in a veil of light and cloak them in a sheet of colour. By covering them in gold heated healing, and lift, with intense concentration, the bad energy from their physical body.

A human body is but a cover. A pretty or unique veil we greet each day, and every single person walking is different, and defined by individual looks. The next step is to exercise the illness or pain with sheer concentration and throw it into the light, or to the soil.

After I have removed this earthbound pain with colour bars and by injection therapy (all from my mind, not physical) I then cover them in white/silver or gold sheets, shielding and holding in the healing work (mentally). The patient may experience a sensation of emotions — tears, heat, exhaustion, relief yet ending in Healing.

166

I perform my healing in an exclusive therapy room in Mayfair, London. Wearing my white doctor's coat, the patient lays on a massage bed in preparation for the therapy. I sit aside on a chair close my eyes and ASK for a white Line Spirit to come close. Then I take the patient's hands in mine, meditate and ask that my hands will be guided by spirit and navigate me to start Healing therapy.

Some patients may need Psychic Surgery, meaning the spirit of a previous surgeon comes in and works through me. My guide is German.

Method: My hands hover over the body to examine, locate the area/s of requiring therapy/surgery. I will also find using my mind the central nerve weakness in the feet and send energy, injection, and bind in gold light.

I am working to find cut and remove illness, pain, cancer, tumour, and so on. The patient is in a relaxed consciousness and completely fine. They may feel absolutely nothing, or hurt from instruments as I am cutting out, or using light works, removing these ailments. I will also place the syringe fashion colour rods or bars to override the disease or pain. After many exercises and procedures has done his work, I am towing all the bad diseases I can see in treatment 1 (of 15) over a period of weeks. I throw this Bad to the ground or soil (mentally) and start to tell the body to REMAP. Remapping is a procedure I developed to tell the body to 'Return' to its original physical self (form) before illness, not unlike plastic when lit. HUMEtherapy, is a mental method to TUNE the visible human body matter, skin, and bone to its former self before the original onset of illness. I feel that illness is earthbound, so by spirit intervention it's possible to remove this energy and remap, returning a smile to a patient.

167

I have had a many patients in my time but there was one that always caught my attention. He was a much older gentleman who had been riddled with cancer, and I was told he would not last a month. I could smell, as I entered the treatment room, his cancer which is like a crippling odour or dumping bags been left outside too long. I gave him a strong, long course of treatment. That was years ago and he is still alive as I write this.

Absent healing can be done by concentration of a client wherever they are on the planet. Using mental visual location and heal by method of either sending light energy or, by placing your mental physical self-there. Moving around the patient and covering them in light, I mentally burn out the area/s of illness. The method to transport myself was something I taught myself back in the eighties. I just found myself about to walk out of my physical self and travel out. I tested this by focusing on a road lamp post at night, and walked up to it turning around 180 degrees, seeing myself in the distance.

THE CODES

CODE 1 — Bullies on Shift

I knew who I was and would not apologise for seeing beyond what my version of dreams and attainment were.

I knew. From the age of 14 I wanted to be a musician (rock star) and I recall a guy in my school called Mathew asking me, "Aren't you worried about exams?"

"Sure, I'll do my best, and better without you near when it's over." I responded. "I am not as worried as you, cos I'm going off to America after school ends..."

One of my key strengths is that I keep to my word and I did pack my bags and produced a plane ticket at the fence where I was catching the coach to the airport. On route to Hollywood while the rest of them were off to double English.

Bullies see their own limitations — I wouldn't dare limit myself, and I had that determination to ensure they wouldn't get the better of me regardless of how loud they shouted.

My CODE for my dear readers here is to visualise yourself away from this situation. Hold onto your identity and worth, you will find it is so much stronger than you think.

CODE 2 — Homelessness

In our lifetimes everyone will go through some hardship. For me, I found it very difficult to believe I was homeless.

Not many people will be homeless in their lifetime but there may be a time where you feel a loss of significant possession of some kind. Once you find yourself in this situation, find the strength and believe it is going to be temporary.

Now, please imagine and visualise a connecting train to where you want to live. You are only here, in this rut, right now while you tidy up things. This is not where you belong but believe and plan the move. Start to look for property in the area you think you belong.

I found myself between 1995-2000 sleeping on so many sofas and temporary flats. Whatever your talent, own it and one day, you can buy your own expensive sofa and feel safe.

If you have been homeless, it is difficult when that ends and you get things. You may obtain possessions and earn more, though all they may grow out and you may feel you want to get rid of some. It may be because you feel you don't deserve them. Have that inner security in you. No-one is coming to ask you to leave, if you are uncomfortable put all the pics on your computer and live like a minimalist.

CODE 3 — Loneliness

It is important to realise that some of us don't have the same destiny and destination as the amazing one we want to have and feel isolated because of this. Others choose what enough for them is. So for those in the former situation, you must take to that room in your head and know you are OK, and that others will recognise and acknowledge you as a talented yet private person. Lonely, yet, you. You must not fear that everyone is looking at you. I learnt they were far too busy to being. So be kind and you will shine far beyond loneliness. All things change — this was just not your time.

CODE 4 — Family

I am from a small family. There were five of us including my aunt and cousin. No dad, but I feel I would not have been as strong to survive if I had one. If you feel alone at times and worse at Christmas, please realise you are the most special one on that day. Christmas is not as significant as it all seems — only TWO hours at the table then, everyone is running for the bar.

Your mum or dad, whoever you relate to are playing their role to protect your future. Yet it is healthy to remark 'why you won't conform and be happy?' Don't try. They will live their life as they will and you the same. Do not wait for permission to be you. Don't get too old that when you are ready to follow your dream, it could be too late.

CODE 5 — Money

Money was always my big issue. It started with the bullies as because of their antics, I always didn't like been part of the crowd or team. I just wanted to save and get to LA, whatever it took.

On the other hand, I never wanted to be in the audience yet on the stage, with some distance from the people. I built a safety mechanism when people get to close. Always know what you truly want even if it seems innocent or late to others. Think to yourself — what are you going to do if you don't have the required skill to get yourself on the path to prosperity? I promise that on your journey, you will learn many things about finance.

Once I had 17 pence to live by for a week. I walked one mile to borrow 20p to buy a stamp to send an application form for a job I truly wanted and with sheer luck and determination, I was offered it. A week later, here I was chatting to Prince Charles alone at my new job on the polo pitch.

Once you put your mind to it, you can succeed financially. For example, if I do thirty readings over a one month period, that will be enough for the ticket to LA. Then it would give me an opportunity to invest in an advert in *LA Weekly* newspaper and stay at Jim's at the Beach hostel for $17 dollars a night. A reading for $150 (80quid) a throw. A couple of those readings and I'd add an open return flight back home.

In the end, I had enough cash to live and do a good job. All in the aid of saving to be a rock star. I would sit in the morning at Jim's and call record labels, make out I had only until Tuesday to meet. Let them fight for you.

Money is a ticket cost plan you mustn't fear. Arrive with a plan then you can have the car, the house.

CODE 6 — Friends

Sometimes, the ones who love you will be there but they are all not destined to join you for the whole ride, but for part of it. Call it life or destiny, we are all born alone really and it's up to us to connect with others along the way.

Cherish the good ones. Others who use you as a canvas, have seen as their limits in life and you happen to be there to take the pieces. They may call you 'selfish' as they may not have wanted, desired or believed enough in their own ability. Be happy alone, there must be something about you that makes you so strong to be okay or alone for a little while. Keep going, friends. Come and change.

CODE 7 — Partners

From the day you meet 'til the day you part, please be you. From the day you meet, don't be controlled — ever. Have your own car keys! Love should, in your heart, always be a bonus you can choose, but not be needy for.

CODE 8 — Survival

I can recall too many times, sadly, that I had to survive things. The choice is to accept the situation, however dark, yet decide that this is not of your creation. Take yourself into that room in your head if you feel despair. Be in your Safe House where you are the focus and kind to your thoughts. Just follow your own heart and all will come up to the light again. It is easier to survive than to jump — that is far harder.

Don't let any one person or moment remove your hope, personality or finish you. You are going to survive and arrive at your desired destination. There are followers and survivors, you just choose the independent route.

Sentimentally, you will be left with tools enabling you to survive things that you once saw as disabling. Yet, what will happen is you will see life as a jewel and see all manner of possibility. Hold your head up, this is just life doing 'life'.

CODE 9 — Depression

Fight it and weather it. Today, you may be lost, hurt, exhausted or worn out yet think to yourself, "I will recover". Live it out. Soon, you may get bored and forget what the issue might have been in the first place. I am not going to take on all they have put upon me. I'm going to find my way out of this temporary tunnel. It can be hard to shift depression so just say to yourself, "I am going to visualise where I want and will be," and take action.

CODE 10 — Legacy

Life can be exactly how we didn't always plan but regardless of the good, bad and indifferent, keep your goal in focus. Do your best and meet someone in your life journey to take your hand. Look to yourself for help mostly. Trust that your goals always belong to you. Create your trademark and never apologise for living. One day you may say, "I'm starting to forget". Don't be sorry, you're healing' Remember, just learn to survive.

AFFIRMATIONS TO REPEAT TO

OVERCOME THESE CODES

1) "Take (back) ownership of myself." This is probably the most important affirmation to healing.
2) "I am going to be better."
3) "My problems are temporary."
4) "This abuse was put upon me, not of my creation."
5) "I will never limit myself."

IN RECORDING

DISCOGRAPHY

Feature tracks & Singles

1986 — Loves Cold Frame as LCC written by LCC produced by-

1987 — INTRUSION as Jolyon

1998 — Nebulablue as Jolyon

2001 — Cold Day in Space, from "Sensyon:Approaching album

2001 — SENSYON, single from Sensyon:Approaching

2003 — Dark Star, from Spirited album as Sensyon

2003 — PLAYOUT, from Spirited album as Sensyon

2005 — Domination (new version appeared on GODMADEMEHARDCORE album produced by THE DROYDS, Richard Norris and Andy Chatterley for Island, as Sensyon

2009 — KilluSexi from Dreams In Flatline, as Jenna Leigh-Raine

2010 — DESERTblonde, from Desert Blonde album, as Jenna Leigh-Raine

2013 — A LOVE KILLING, from Onyx album double A-side single will include-B-side track"INK- (to be finalised)

Feb 2014 — Why Cry Now

Jan 2016 — Rebel Still Runs

As Sensyon

1987 — Demos LA I'm coming home
1994 — Sound for Aliens album, written and produced by Jolyon in Fulham
1996 — Music Jolyanna (best of) includes single for Samantha Kelly 'ICON', written produced by Jolyon
2000 — TYLO album, written and produced by Jolyon
2001 — Sensyon:Approaching album, written and produced by Sensyon
2003 — Spirited album, written and produced by Sensyon
2005 — Sensyon Airways, 20th anniversary double album includes Domination 2, by Island Records

Jenna Leigh-Raine — Album projects

2009 — Dreams In Flatline
2010 — Afterlife (MAXI) 3Track
2010 — DESERTblonde
2013 — Onyx
2016 — Errās (Film Project) 5-Track
2017 — NOMA (for EML)
2017 — MESSAGEZ

All music projects

1982 — First lyrics written
1986 — Single *Love Cold Frame*, co-produced by Ray Hedges at the Padded Cell Recording Studios in Colnblook. Written by Richard Mills.

Recorded several other tracks including a live recording LCC at Slough Town Football Club on November 8th, 1986

1987 — First solo recording was lost, though updated version of *Intrusion* (re-recorded) appears on first solo album SFA. Other track, Stage (produced by Jolyon) lost, though re-recorded for another artist.

1989 — Recorded tracks for producer Tim Autman for WEA Paris/ USA Lost Demos

1993-4 — Additional track and mix by Jonny Male of Republica though, part of Soul Family sensation at the time and solo contract was signed to One Little Indian in York Road. Published 15-track album.

Tracks

1) Masters; 2) Noise; 3) Intrusion; 4) Natural Time; 5) All I Did; 6) Buddyface; 7) Tempt; 8) New Y Punk; 9) First Poison 10) Waterfall 11) Sound for Aliens 12) What's Your Poison 13) Moon River 14) Stargazing* 15) In Front of the World

* Extra version of STARGAZING APPEARS ON MUSIC JOLYANNA 1998 ALBUM

1994 — First solo album *Sound for Aliens*. Written, arranged, performed and produced by Jolyon, engineered by Alex McGowan at Fulham Rectory Studios, Fulham Palace.

1994 — A four-year project creating an album compilation released in 1998, called *Music Jolyanna* with new tracks. All music and words were by Jolyon, additional tracks recorded in Southside Studios in Clapham for Intrusion Records, engineered by Pete Barraclough.

Tracks

1) Spacebaby; 2) Stargazing 2; 3) Domination (Original VN); 4) A Little Attention (Early VOX); 5) Passionatta; 6) What's Your Poison (Private Dancer Mix)

1997 — Lost Recordings, from Limosine Sessions

1997 — Three-track single created for Samantha Kelly. Everything had been done by Jolyon at Forgotten Records in Fulham Broadway.

1997 — Track *Vertigo* a demo with Jonny Male

1998 — Single *Nebulablue*. Written, arranged, performed and produced by Jolyon. Mix Engineering and additional guitar by Pete Barraclough.

1998 — Compilation CD album, by peoplesound.com in 20 Orange Street, London WC2H 7ED. ALBUM CAT NO. ART 1568-CD01

Tracks

1) Nebulablue 3.27; 2) Domination (Original VN) 3.54; 3) Passionatta 4.05; 4) A Little Attention 3.27; 5) Icon (feat. Samantha Kelly) 3.31; 6) Stargazing 2.44; 7) Noise 2.53; 8) Tempt 2.23; 9) Sound for Aliens 3.47; 10) Spacebaby 3.45; 11) Waterfall 3.03

2000 — On February 25th, produced four-track demo CD for Label Interest for forthcoming album, Tylo.

Demo Tracks

1) Tylo; 2) The Messenger; 3) Red (Instrumental VN) 4) Tylo (Movement Zero)

Album Tracks

1) Tylo; 2) Hermes; 3) Telepsy; 4) Report; 5) Idaho; 6) Red; 7) Electra; 8) Molecular; 9) Idaho (The Overture)

2001 — Album Sensyon:Approaching (see all pictures as reference). All words and music by Sensyon (Jolyon), recorded in Siobhan's home between 2001 and 2002 in Belsize Park.

Tracks

1) Sensyon Approaching 1.24; 2) Sensyon 3.21; 3) Blonde on Black 4.10; 4) Cold Day in Space 3.21; 5) Windows (Piano Movement 1) 3.37; 6) Playtime 3.41; 7) Exhibition 0.50; 8) Dark Star 2.52; 9) Platinum 3.18; 10) Departure 3.35; 11) Departure Time 2.15; 12) Sensyon (Point 0800 Degrees) 1.53

2002 — Additional tracks were added to Sensyon:Approaching. Cheerleader Remix by Richard Mills in Colnbrook.

Tracks

1) Playout 2) In Future Affection 3) In Future Affection (Instrumental) 4) Playout (Cheerleader Remix)

2002 — *Blonde on Black* appears on Mayhem, a new compilation for Matchbox Recordings.

2003 — Album, Spirited, by Sensyon and mixed by Richard Mills in Bath Road, near Heathrow in Berkshire.

Tracks

1) Kindred; 2) Xsport; 3) Domination (New VN); 4) Lovechild; 5) Playout; 6) Tanned; 7) Beautiful Darkness; 8) Send in Devon; 9) In Future Affection; 10) Take a Lifetime; 11) Her Parade; 12) Spirited

2005 — Domination was re-recorded by Richard Norris and Andy Chatterley for The Electro Album 'God Give Me Hardcore' for Island.

2005 — Album compilation, Sensyon Airways was released.

Tracks

1) Blonde on Black; 2) Stargazing; 3) Intrusion; 4) Dominations (for Island); 5) Tylo; 6) Tanned; 7) Tempt; 8) Playout; 9) Waterfall; 10) Idaho (The Overture); 11) Departure; 12) Electra; 13) Lovechild; 14) Xsport; 15)

Windows (First Movement 1); 16) Nebulablue; 17) In Future Affection; 18) Spirited; 19) Sensyon; 20) Why Cry Now (Final Call 05)

2009 — Album, Dreams in Flatline, by Jenna Leigh-Raine, recorded in Chelsea, London.

Tracks

1) Execute 3.24; 2) Glazed Over 0.54; 3) Glaze 3.54; 4) Kill U Sexi 6.25; 5) Dirty Hazard Hate 4.37; 6) NewPornChic 3.42; 7) Dark Lolita 3.31; 8) Elegant Black 2.25; 9) Dreams in Flatline 3.33; 10) Razed 4.06; 11) Redsoul 4.26; 12) Sensy-tiv 4.41; 13) Midium 1.03; 14) My Love 3.36; 15) Indian 3.39; 16) Dark Rift 2.46

2009 — Instrumental album, Afterlife, was recorded in Realtime on September 17th. Written, composed, arranged, performed and produced by Jenna, assisted engineering by Richard Mills. Copyright owned by EML UK Electronic Music Library, Christopher Payne and Nigel Mates for EML.

Tracks

1) Ghosts in the House (Formerly *Presence 2*); 2) Soul Walker; 3) Afterlife

2010 — Mini-album, DESERTblonde was released. Written, arranged, performed and produced by Jenna. Recorded in Chelsea, London and appeared online and BBC Introducing.

Tracks

1) Erased; 2) DESERTblonde; 3) Fallen; 4) Blanket; 5) Personal; 6) Xperienced 2

2013 — Album, Onyx, was released. Written, arranged, performed, produced and mix-engineered by Jenna. Pre-mastered in Archway, London and Surrey. Final mastering limited by Jenna Leigh-Raine / DAZ Shields.

Tracks

1) In Stitches; 2) Onyx; 3) Dirty Machine; 4) Do or Die; 5) Dirty Machine (Maverick); 6) Hotfuss; 7) Ink; 8) Actress; 9) Humanway; 10) Positioned and Palace; 11) A Love Killing; 12) Hidden; 13) Before Time Dies; 14) Dirty Machine (Extended)

2013 — The production of Killerbody, compilation of Jenna's work between 2008 and 2013.

Tracks

1) Execute; 2) Personal; 3) Newpornchic; 4) Afterlife; 5) Redsoul; 6) Kill U Sexi; 7) Fallen; 8) Midium My-Love; 9) Sensy-tiv; 10) Dark Lolita; 11) DESERTblonde; 12) Darkrift; 13) Blanket; 14) Erazed; 15) Glaze; 16) Idaho (The Overture)

2016 — Film Score Music Entitled 'Per Aspera Ad Astra'.

Tracks

Per Ardua Ad Astra 2) Endrah 3) Tollunt 4) Errās 5) Per Aspera Ad Astra 6) Gama

2016 — The release of album 'STATIC' for EML

Tracks

1) Dark Room; 2) Ascension; 3) Warm Sun Up; 4) Redemption Plan 7; 5) Progress Orb; 6) Reform; 7) Soul Replay; 8) Descender; 9) Travel Static; 10) Loud Silent; 11) Empire Sun; 12) Noma; 13) No Repeat

2017 — Album in working progress 'MESSAGEZ'

Tracks

1) Importance of Being Zero; 2) Ethics (If it's Gonna Happen); 3) Maine (What Matters Now); 4) 7D; 5) Brave Shadow; 6) Last Riots; 7) If We Finish (If I Fall); 8) Hospital; 9) Black Flame; 10) Messagez

Notes

Any other tracks were either lost or forgotten.

All tracks written – word and music – by Jenna Leigh-Raine, in all names listed or otherwise where stated.

Other tracks, affiliation and mixes titles from various albums as listed.

From 'Sound for Aliens' album, extra song versions were made: 1) Intrusion (The French Connection, long-play and live mix) 23/9/1993; 2) Intruder (Intro) live version; 3) Valley Valley (new Y-version) instrumental live use; 4) Buddyface (reprise) live use plus demo version 17/7/1994; 5) Learn the Corruption (May 1994)

Sensyon:Approaching album extras: 1) Platinum star / Platinum (hidden track as appears end 0.5 album; 2) Sensyon:Point 0800 degrees

Jenna Leigh-Raine appears courtesy of multiple / singer, composer, producer, multi-instrumentalist, keyboards, drums, programming, synths, pianos, guitars.

All information related to recordings above are as accurate to, and from, original master tapes, records and CDs.

EPILOGUE

To me, the book is about survival over odds that on paper should not be possible. Though, with several virtual safe houses I built inside my mind, I lived through it all. With these tools, I learnt how to cope and survive.

The book is an in-depth travel log of countries, situations and challenges. Yet, it is a fun, rock 'n' roll journey with soundtrack. It is not based on just one or two areas of my life. Rather, every dark and light avenue to get to and back to my passion and path — in music.

It may be the first of its kind and reads unforgivingly, about true version of events. Fun, sad and wild, right until the story's end — I give in to these truths. I bare my life trials and knowledge to show anyone the afraid 12-year-old who said 'you can be anything you want'.

It touches on such elements of my life — from my torturous school-hood, to my battles in the music business, to launching a successful career as a psychic, model, adult film producer, and to hanging out with amazing celebs, plus much more.

In Stitches definition: a play on three hidden wrapped meanings that sums up my turmoil, triumph and bloody times starting in Rio in 1976 to the present day. Here, I lift the lid on forty years in the most incredible life I never want to repeat, forget or change.

I never planned this magical alternative life. All I ever really wanted was for my music to be centre, but so it seemed I was put in-front of the music. Not to hide, but to live as my real self and maybe the music will play loud as I start to forget.

Never let life limit you, and angels will watch over 'til you're happy.

19238855R00111

Printed in Poland
by Amazon Fulfillment
Poland Sp. z o.o., Wrocław